Management for Professionals

More information about this series at
http://www.springer.com/series/10101

Johannes Robier

UX Redefined

Winning and Keeping Customers with Enhanced Usability and User Experience

Springer

Johannes Robier
youspi Consulting GmbH
Graz, Austria

ISBN 978-3-319-21061-2 ISBN 978-3-319-21062-9 (eBook)
DOI 10.1007/978-3-319-21062-9
Springer Cham Heidelberg Dordrecht London New York

Library of Congress Control Number: 2015945941

Originally published in German with the title "Das einfache und emotionale Verkaufserlebnis. Mit Usability, User Experience und Customer Experience anspruchsvolle Kunden gewinnen" published by Springer Gabler in 2015 with ISBN 978-3-658-10129-9

Printed on acid-free paper

Springer International Publishing is part of Springer Science+Business Media
(www.springer.com)

Preface

What is the customer's motivation to buy my product?

What is the customer's reason to use my service?

Why should I invest in a company?

"The Reason to Believe" is the persuasive *motive to buy*. It constitutes the main reason why products are bought, services are used and why customers are turned into loyal brand evangelists.

In its essence, "The Reason to Believe" has the purpose of confirming the customer's purchase choice through actual and subjectively perceived facts, thereby boosting and strengthening customer satisfaction and loyalty. Moreover, "The Reason to Believe" provides a good feeling for the customer, reinforcing the belief of having made the right choice, which in turn sparks product recommendation as well. Without a compelling 'reason to believe' your product will remain unnoticed.

This book equips you with hands-on tools to create, communicate and ultimately boost your products and services. "The Reason to Believe" walks you not only through the psychological basics of information dissemination, but provides methodic and usable applications as well.

Do not be mistaken and assume "The Reason to Believe" has to constitute your product's uniqueness, equaling its unique selling proposition. The truth is, the customer's actual reason to buy products might as well be personal appreciation, trust in a single person, or simply a conveyed emotion. Hence, "The Reason to Believe" and a product's uniqueness are two different concepts.

Contrary to common belief, customers purchase primarily because of the "The Reason to Believe" – and not because of a product's uniqueness. However, it cannot be excluded that in some cases both may be the same.

Contents

"The Reason to Believe"? 1

The first chapter deals with the principles of information preparation with the aim of gaining an understanding of how people perceive the environment, how information should be prepared, and which issues we will have to engage with more deeply if we are to create buying experiences. We will work through the physiological preconditions to get to the point at which we know how information should be processed in a manner consistent with the workings of the brain. We will also review the definitions of terms used in the industry in order to arrive at a common understanding of what they mean. Here we will make a clear distinction between usable, user-friendly (usability), user experience, and customer experience.

It's a Wednesday afternoon and I am sitting in my office and working on a new software concept for a client. The software's complexity is demanding my full attention and I can feel a proper solution is about to be found.

Suddenly my phone rings, diverting my attention and pulling me out of the design. It's my grandmother and having already lost my concentration, I answer the call, of course.

"Hannes, I want to buy a computer, so I can access the Internet. My friends tell me to go on the Internet and chat with them – so what exactly is an 'Internet chat'? Can you find me the right computer?"

What will I recommend? What's "The Reason to Believe" in this case? **Have you ever found yourself in a similar situation?**

You are planning a vacation in the near future. You envision yourself spending your time off work on a beautiful location close to the sea. Thus, you access an online search engine and type in "hotel by the sea." The first results page already presents you with a multitude of websites and you visit the first few pages and quickly decide on two vacation portals.

Have you ever wondered why you made this decision? What was the "The Reason to Believe"? What are these two websites offering that the others did not?

You browse the two vacation portals to find a suitable hotel, using four different filters. Your final choices are comprised of five hotels. Which one will you book? What is the actual "Reason to Believe"?

J. Robier, *UX Redefined*, Management for Professionals, DOI 10.1007/978-3-319-21062-9_1

A company is in need of a new software product. Three different providers are invited to pitch their offer. Every sales manager explains that his product is the best one available on the market. Each presented product meets all the previously stated demands, offers a multitude of additional functionalities and showcases a respectable list of references.

Which product is most likely to be chosen?

Many customers will decide in favor of the product with the simplest design – even if that means certain functionalities may be sacrificed. They will have a closer look at the product, reflect on whether they understand it and think about how much training time will be required to completely use it. Simplicity and perceived "ease of use" wins. Why do we decide this way?

You are finally taking the city trip that you have been looking forward to and long preparing for. Having finally reached your destination of choice you realize the information signs are anything but easily comprehensible or even nonexistent. Therefore, to be safe, you choose to take an expensive taxi to get to your hotel, even though you are an advocate of public transport.

What made you change your mind and go for the taxi service?

The next day you are all set for an exciting city tour. You are walking from one attraction to the next, ending up on a street packed with lovely cafés. **Which one will go you for? What will be your "Reason to Believe" in this context?**

You are all set to buy a new printer within the retail market. Given that you are not familiar with any of the brands and do not know what to look for, you seek advice from a sales clerk and proudly end up buying the recommended printer. At home, you unpack the new product and as promised it all seems very easy to use: unpack the printer, plug in the power cord, the USB cable and get ready to print. However, something is not working out and after three full hours of reading and attempting to follow the manual's instructions, you give up.

Why did you decide on the printer in the first place? Did the product manage to keep its promise and were your expectations met?

You are looking for a talent who should perfectly complement your existing team: a tech-savvy, creative thought leader with comprehensive sales skills. You want to make sure to reach out to potentials by using a variety of media including online platforms, a headhunter, as well as print media to promote the vacant position. After only a few weeks you have five very interesting candidates on your shortlist, but after the next round of interviews only two people remain. Both showcase similar high-quality references and a comprehensive know-how. The only slight difference is while one appears to have more profound technical skills, the other one has served in an honorary capacity in his leisure time. While the technical expertise of the first candidate clearly provides an advantage, you appreciate the voluntary work of the second candidate, which might reflect a greater tendency to commitment. Whom will you choose?

Do any of these situations sound familiar to you? Are you confronted with similar questions from time to time?

All situations and examples discussed within the following sections are built on concepts of communication and information assimilation. To better understand these and to be able to draw valid conclusions, we will first discuss the fundamentals of information intake.

1.1 Fundamentals of Information Reception

Elderly people in particular often feel a bit overwhelmed with the wealth of options and information we are currently confronted with. Consequently we often hear phrases such as, "Back in our days, everything was much simpler". In fact, this statement holds a great deal of truth.

30 years ago, a TV had a power switch and two or three channels to watch. Therefore, the options and transmitted information was relatively simple to understand and easy to manage. Today, however, we utilize comprehensive remote controls offering 300 different functions and thousands of television programs that can be accessed on the internet. An even more startling development is being showcased in telecommunications: the first mobile phones had massive cases, keypads and long antennas. Today, they are small and thin multi-function smart devices that go far beyond their basic task of enabling us to make a telephone call.

It is ours, as well as future generations' challenge to consolidate the mass amounts of information and prepare it in a way that makes it comprehensible and usable for individuals. Regardless of how much information humanity generates within a year, human receptiveness has no chance of keeping up pace. Indeed, we start to disregard unnecessary information, as showcased through the "banner blindness" meaning, we tend to ignore advertisements on the Internet, as we focus our minds on the content of websites.

Note

In 2002 five exabytes of information was stored on paper, in films, as well as magnetic and optical storages. This amounts roughly to the amount of all words ever spoken by mankind. In addition, it is noteworthy to mention that every person produced approximately 800 megabyte of stored information throughout the course of a year, which amounts to about ten meters book, if it were to be stored on paper. Multiplying these numbers by 6,3 billion, you can start to sense a relation that corresponds to humanity.

These numbers increase every year (Berkeley 2003).

Out of the ten million bit sensory perceptions (seeing, hearing, smelling, feeling, tasting) per second, only about 16 bit make it to our ultra-short-term memory. They are then stored for about ten to twenty seconds unconsciously before disappearing again from our awareness.

We only notice and remember information, when our attention is being drawn to it during these ten to twenty seconds and out of the 16 bit, only 0,5–0,7 bit per second can be passed on to the short-term memory, Fig. 1.1. There, the information gets stored for a couple of minutes, if it does not get further attention. If the information reception is being repeated or perceived as very important at this point, it can be passed on into the long-term memory. This information conversion is influenced and supported primarily through repetition, emotion, and connection with various

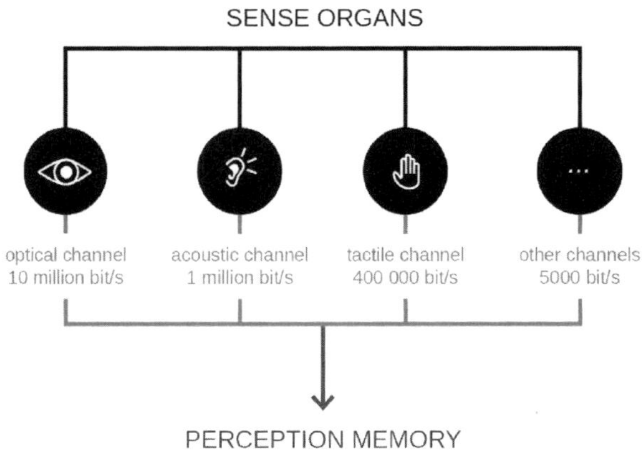
SENSE ORGANS
optical channel
10 million bit/s
acoustic channel
1 million bit/s
tactile channel
400 000 bit/s
other channels
5000 bit/s
PERCEPTION MEMORY

Fig. 1.1 Perception Memory. (source: Schilling 1993)

sensory perceptions (Herczeg 1994a). The capacity of the short-term memory is about seven data units (Herczeg 1994b).

Example

Look at the words below for a maximum of 20 seconds and attempt to memorize as many as possible:

Chemistry	Attention	Door	Only	Church
Idea	Various	Cloth	Grass	Father
Opinion	Screw	Behavior	Walk	Circle
Until	Ring	Woman full	Limit	

How many words were you able to memorize?

In order to store information, our awareness plays an essential role. This principle implies that the short-term memory can store approximately five to nine units (seven ± two) when it comes to pre-known Information and three to five units (four ± one) when it comes to new information (Miller 1956).

From this, the optimal number of menu items or bullet points can be derived for information processing.

How do you memorize a combination of numbers?

1. If you repeat the combination often and keep repeating it. This allows the information to be passed on to the long-term memory.
2. If you connect this combination with an emotion or an experience, like the birth date of a dear friend.

Whenever we steer our awareness on specific information, we manage to memorize it.

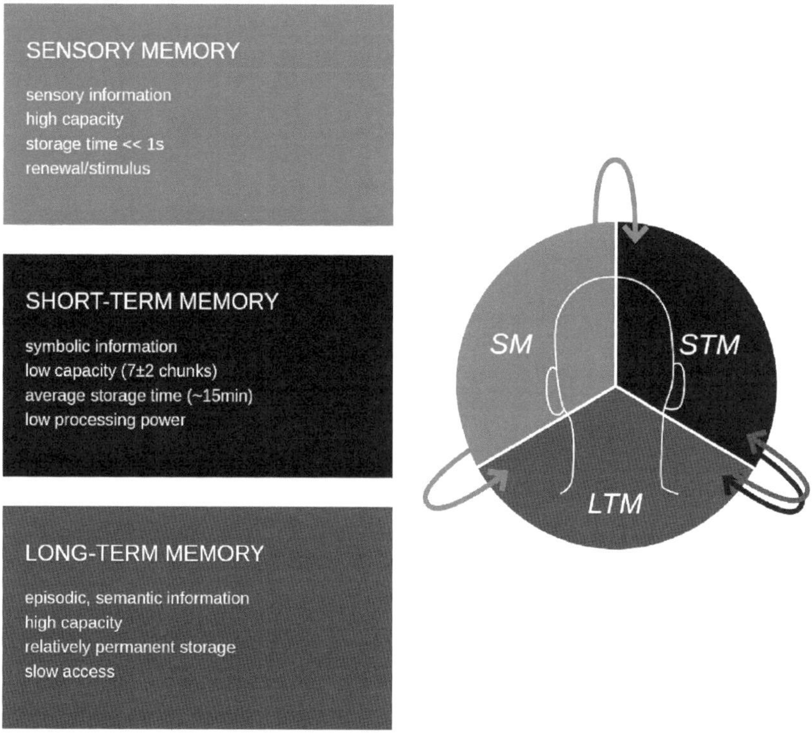
SENSORY MEMORY
sensory information
high capacity
storage time << 1s
renewal/stimulus
SHORT-TERM MEMORY
symbolic information
low capacity (7±2 chunks)
average storage time (~15min)
low processing power
LONG-TERM MEMORY
episodic, semantic information
high capacity
relatively permanent storage
slow access
SM
STM
LTM

Fig. 1.2 One Perception-Reaction Cycle takes about 70 ms (1/14 s)

The following factors activate our awareness (Heineken and Habermann 1994)

- Alienation,
- Humor,
- Exaggeration,
- Surprise,
- Triggering Personal Consternation.

► In general, the following applies: the more senses are involved in information perception, the more information will be stored.

Clearly, we are not able to process the ten million bit sensory perceptions that we are confronted with. Fig. 1.2 However, training and exercises allow us to optimize our receptivity.

Given the information overload we are confronted with on a daily basis, it is no surprise that many decisions are being made without questioning details.

Many products and services, as well as advertising messages are designed by companies and don't reflect human needs which in turn, becomes a burden for end users who make their way through massive amounts of information clutter. This burden subsequently means that the target audience will not make use of or actively perceive information and as a consequence, the company's economic situation will suffer.

Thus arise:

- Products that are not needed,
- Unsatisfied customers,
- Hurdles to use,
- Confusing Service Processes,
- Low "Returns on Investments".

Albert Einstein said:

> If you can't explain it simply, you don't understand it well enough.

Hence, products and services need user-friendly (usability) designs, which means a

Customer-oriented Process Optimization

for services, products and information.

How can we design information in such a way that it will be perceived and accepted?

Many product and service developments are based on technical or legal requirements and often cannot be circumvented. However, let's take one step back to the very beginning of proper design.

Which tools are available to design information?

From a technical point of view, the binary system is the easiest way to transmit information. Due to our limited storage capacity, it is very difficult to remember binary numerical orders and decipher them. Do you know the meaning of the numbers below?

01010111011001010110111001101110001000000110010101110011001

00000011001010110100101101110011001100110000101100011011010

00001000000111011111100100011100100110010100100000010010010
11011100110011001101111011100100110101011000010111010001100

10010110111101101110011001010110111000100000011110100111010

10010000001110110011001010111001001110011011101000110010101

10100001100101011011100010110000100000011001000110000101101

11001101110001000000110011111100100011000100110010100100000
01100101011100110010000001101011011001010110100101101110011
00101001000000100101101101111011011010110110101110101011011

10011010010110101101100001011101000110100101101111011011100

11100110111000001110010011011110110001001101100011001010110
11010110010100100000011000010111010101100110001000000111010

10110111001110011011001010111001001100101011100100010000001

01011101100101011011000111010000101110001000000101010101110

01101100001011000100110100101101100011010010111010001111001
00100000001001100010000001010011011010010110110101110000011

01100011010010110001101101001011101000111100100100000011010

000110010101101001011100110111001101110100001000000011011100

110100101100011011010000111010001110011001000000011000010110
11100110010001100101011100100110010101110011001011000010000
00110000101101100011100110010000001001001011011100110011001
10111101110010011011010110000101110100011010010110111101101

110011001010110111000100000011100110110111100100000001100001

01110101011001100111101001110101011000100110010101110010011
00101011010010111010001100101011011100010110000100000011001

00011000010111001101110011001000000110010101110011001000000

110010001100101011100100010000000100010101101110011001000110

10110111010101101110011001000110010100100000001011110010000
001010101011100110110010101110010001000000011101100110010101

110010011100110111010001100101011010000111010000101110

For humans it is almost impossible to remember the above numbers. Have you ever seen an advertisement composed of binary numbers?

> This means: 'If it was easy to understand information, then there would be communication problems in our world. Usability and Simplicity mean nothing other than designing information in a way to enable the end-user/customer to understand it.'

The next option is to minimize the number of binary numbers through representing them as hexadecimal numbers. Thence we can remember the information more easily since we do not have to deal with such a vast amount of numbers any longer.

Mnemonics function is very similar. We attempt to present, structure and convey information in an easier way by setting an anchor with something familiar. Look at the mnemonic for a waxing or waning moon:

DOC represents this:

"D" – Waxing Moon
"O" – Full Moon
"C" – Waning Moon

Table 1.1 Digital encoding of information

Binary	Hexadecimal	Decimal
1111 =	F =	15
1.1111 =	1F =	31
11.0111.1100.0101 =	37C5 =	14.277
1010.1100.1101.1100 =	ACDC =	44.252

En- and decoding information helps our short-term memory to better perceive and store information. How often have you seen ads with hexadecimals? The smaller the amount of information, the longer and better we can remember it, Table 1.1.

The storage period of one information unit is about 130 seconds. If the units are increased and we have to process three units, the storage period – Fig. 1.3 – decreases to only fifteen seconds (Preim 1999, see also Preim 1999, S. 183 f).

What is the optimal form to convey information?

Let's have a closer look at the fundamentals of human physiology. When we pay attention to how information is perceived through our sensory organs, we can draw various inferences.

More than 80 percent of the information we receive is being perceived through our eyes. Storing and converting these perceived images constitutes sixty percent of our brain activity (Gegenfurtner et al. 2002).

Since the eye is the main information carrier, images are captured directly. In contrast, text is an encrypted type of information that we have to learn to decipher with great effort in our childhood. An image, a facial expression and gestures can be processed and interpreted worldwide, although corresponding meanings may vary due to cultural differences.

Our language, in turn, is a fundamental human listening experience. In fact, since Ancient times we have shared and communicated through language and pinned sounds. Here, however, we do not yet distinguish between different languages and writing. The encoding of language into text was only developed at a much later stage.

The importance of images is physiologically supported by the fact that our visual center in the brain is closely connected with other brain regions. Thus, the image of a sunrise may address and evoke a range of emotions and stored information within us. Example: Envision a magnificent and picturesque sunrise:

Magnificent and Picturesque Sun Rise

What are you seeing? What feelings have been evoked? What memories are connected to these words?

Every person has a different set of memories and emotions and will draw upon a multitude of experiences, connections and knowledge upon being presented with this sentence. This is based on the fact that all of these are tied to the image of a sunrise.

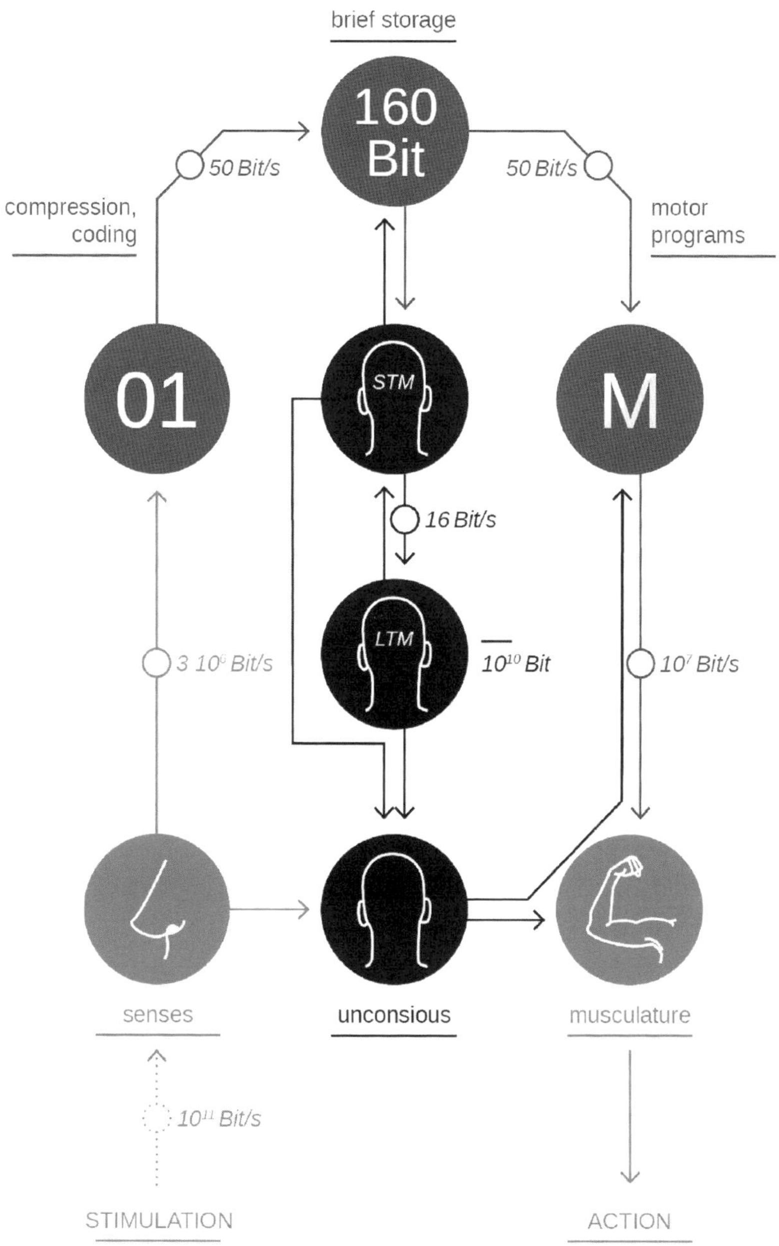
brief storage
160 Bit
50 Bit/s
50 Bit/s
compression, coding
motor programs
01
STM
M
16 Bit/s
LTM
3 10⁶ Bit/s
10¹⁰ Bit
10⁷ Bit/s
senses
unconsious
musculature
10¹¹ Bit/s
STIMULATION
ACTION

Fig. 1.3 Brain Processing; see also Schorpp 2015

Fig. 1.4 Picture of a sunrise

AQUATA
Erfrischend. Belebend. Gesund.

Fig. 1.5 Student work in art class

When we exchange the words for an image, the image's effect can be enhanced by up to ten times (Scheier and Held 2006).

What is it that you see now in Fig. 1.4? What are you feeling now? What memories are connected to the sunrise above?

Images take on a fundamental role in the processing of information and can strongly impact the pace of a customer in understanding and accepting information. This is among the reasons why graphics, images and a vivid visual language are integrated in diverse products. Advertising is mainly based on imagery. As images are quickly absorbed by our brain they can easily convey emotions. Typically, the message will be reinforced and enhanced through text and thus complex information can be conveyed more directly, Fig. 1.5.

Try to pay attention to your surroundings and look for the many occasions, where images are used. Where can you find a lack of images? Why are no images being used there?

We are now getting closer to understanding optimal information processing. What does a brain-conform presentation of information look like?

1.2 Brain-Conform Information

Due to the enormous increase of information in our society, it is not a surprise that our future is getting more and more complex. Every day we face a greater amount of information and challenges. Customers will stop perceiving and understanding a lot of available information, as the half-life of information seems to decrease by half every year. It is increasingly difficult to understand the scope of technology and functionalities and likewise, it gets more difficult to compare or select from an available product range.

I am often confronted with the question, "which laptop is currently state-of-the-art and is the best performing product?" An easy-to-answer question? If you are not keeping up with the latest developments, processors and details, it can be quite tough to determine which model to choose.

Let's simplify this question by looking at the people, who pose it. Most often people who ask me for this advice need a solid office product, want to surf the web and write emails. We can match these requirements with the technical performance of current notebooks. It is safe to say that virtually every laptop currently on the market will meet these requirements. Was it difficult to find this answer?

For this reason, the simplification of information will be further integrated into our daily lives. Nevertheless, it will still be possible to counteract. I will show you how to design information for the target audience in an intuitive, receivable, simple and emotional way making it brain-conform.

Information always has an end, as information is comprised solely of bits and bytes. Emotions only arise in our minds and only through emotions is our interest peeked. For this reason all information needs to be either

1. Simple
   In order for people to pick it up and understand it instantly. This holds especially true for products, processes and services in our everyday work lives, as work needs to be done in an efficient and rapid manner. User hurdles entail inefficiency. Simplicity is also key in advertising – the target audience has to understand and process the message within seconds. Or:
2. Emotional
   There must be emotion in order for people to feel addressed and motivated. This is of particular importance and touches the areas of marketing, advertising and general design of information. The first impression is critical when it comes to the ultimate purchase decision.

In fact, whenever emotional needs are addressed, information also has to be simple in order for it to be directly perceived. This leads us to:

3. Simple and Emotional

Let's draw our attention to an important fact: **We cannot spark emotions or direct interest for our information within other people.** Such interest is always self-motivated and peeks within the respective person looking at the information. For this reason we can only create the conditions and the right setting to evoke emotions and spark interest.

- If you are single and are being offered, via an advertisement, an engagement ring on Facebook, you will hardly notice the advertisement
- A newsletter that will not fit into your field of interest will most likely be deleted before you have even perceived the entire subject line, or will lead to an immediate un-subscription, if you open it

Through simplicity in processes and emotionality, motivation is triggered within us, or in many cases demotivation and the consequent 'information blindness' can be circumvented.

> Our brain only works through
> motivation and interest.

We work, think, become creative and propose solutions for everyday situations or for professional applications.

> We all are capable of learning, but inconvincible;
> We all do not learn when we have to learn, but when we want to learn;
> We change our behavior only,
> When we choose to do so ourselves,
> And when we see the actual reason (Siebert 1998).

BRAIN CONFORM information means:

SIMPLE = Reducing to the essentials within the context of experience of tasks, in order to enable us to process information more rapidly (Usability).

or

EMOTIONAL = Creating connections in order to store information more easily and facilitate the conversion into long-term memory (Experience).

When both areas are combined, we refer to the "user experience" or "customer experience" of products, services or even entire businesses when these connotations get integrated into the overall corporate strategy.

Given that completely different job profiles have arisen within these areas, looking at these two concepts in greater detail and discussing the differences is essential. This is paramount in order to grasp the connections and linkage between the various subject areas.

1.3 Usability vs User Experience

By definition, usability is all about developing products efficiently, effectively and to the highest satisfaction of the customer, Fig. 1.6. However, these three properties should not only be applied to products, but also extended to services and processes to create and design holistic experiences.

The area of User Experience has tapped into this approach and puts even more of an emphasis on the inclusion of all customer processes that lead to and follow the usage of a product in the design process. User experience comprises various industries and areas. If one must pin user experience to three key topics, they would be the following: Definition, Understanding, Communication, Fig. 1.7.

In order to comprehensively prepare and design products and processes, one must divide the user experience of products and processes in three phases: the definition phase, the communication phase and the phase of understanding.

Products and services need to offer more than simply being average – they should provide the user with an overall positive experience. This includes the design and

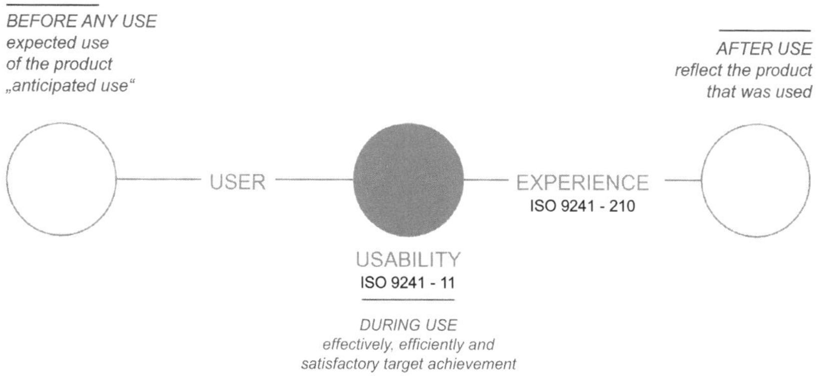
BEFORE ANY USE
expected use
of the product
„anticipated use“
AFTER USE
reflect the product
that was used
USER
EXPERIENCE
ISO 9241 - 210
USABILITY
ISO 9241 - 11
DURING USE
effectively, efficiently and
satisfactory target achievement

Fig. 1.6 Definition of Usability and User Experience

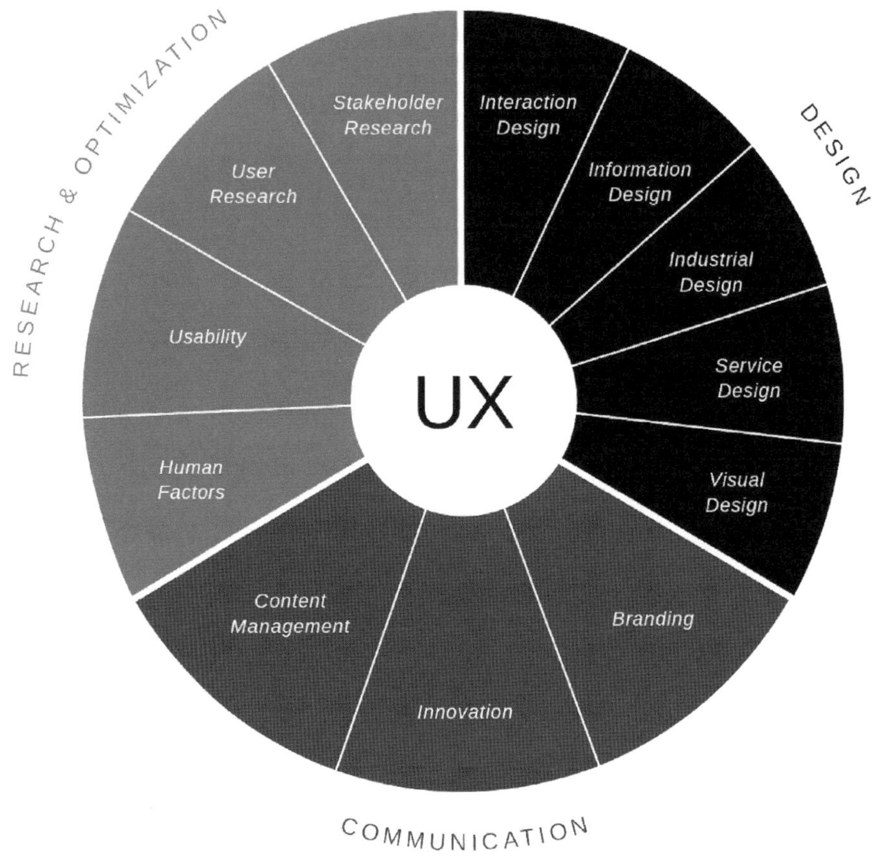
RESEARCH & OPTIMIZATION
DESIGN
COMMUNICATION
UX
Stakeholder Research
Interaction Design
User Research
Information Design
Industrial Design
Usability
Service Design
Human Factors
Visual Design
Content Management
Branding
Innovation

Fig. 1.7 Definition of User Experience

an emotional experience before, during and after any interaction with the product or service.

Example: The purchase of a bouquet of flowers for Mother's Day. Usability focuses on the website – surfing the web, selection within a set of possible choices, making one's way through the purchase process and finally the order confirmation page.

User Experience takes it one step further by looking at the processes before and after these activities. Is there a flyer that will promote the website? What does the primary in-store contact look like, does it promote the website? Are there any marketing measures such as online promotions? Therefore the complete user experience looks at the entire journey from product search to the actual product arrival at its final destination including, as well, the transportation and packaging process.

All topics and areas form parts play a role in the user experience and alter it. Hence, user experience is a very broad field. Taking it one step further and comparing user experience to the concept of customer experience, we learn that here, an even more holistic approach is applicable.

1.4 Customer Experience

Customer experience takes the next step by managing and merging all touch points between a company and the customer.

In addition to user experience, customer experience also looks at the internal processes. When employees adopt a customer-oriented mindset and present information in the correct way, as well as endorse the philosophy of customer experience, they also manage to serve customers in the best possible way.

In order for employees to be able to create experiences, every employee needs to adhere to a certain set of rules and also be aware of his freedom. This will empower him to take the right actions during customer contact, in new situations, or when being confronted with complaints. In addition, those employees without direct customer contact represent a large target group of customer experience, as well. Through their contacts with friends and relatives, they are the first carrier of a company's philosophy and values. Word-of-mouth marketing from such reliable sources lies among the fundamentals of a well-functioning company.

A service employee with direct contact to the end customer has to act according to clearly defined rules. Nevertheless, it is indispensable for this employee to have specific freedoms within his framework.

Let's assume you receive a rental device for free whenever you purchase a certain number of corresponding products from a company. For an event, you make use of this offer, but unfortunately, part of the device is broken, leading to resentment with event participants. You call customer service to let them know about your complaint, so they offer you a free rental device for the next time you need one. For you, this does not alleviate the negative experienced, as you can get the rental device for free anyway because of the large number of corresponding products you buy from this company.

The customer support clerk tells you that there is nothing he can do at this point and apologizes. Now you feel even more upset, because not only was the machine delivered to you broken, but clearly was the company's fault, and nothing was done to make up for this negative experience. The company's guidelines do not allow for any other way of making up for the broken device. You will not only refrain from buying from this company in the future, but you will be keen on sharing this story with others.

Designing and implementing service processes for all potential situations that may arise with the aim of boosting customer loyalty is just one of the many areas related to Customer Experience Management.

What would have happened if the service team would have had a viable solution from the moment you expressed your dissatisfaction? Most likely even a small make up gesture would have been sufficient and you would have been satisfied since your needs and concerns would have been heard and alleviated. The costs for the company would not have been noteworthy.

To better illustrate the connection between User Experience and Customer Experience, please have a closer look at the graph in Fig. 1.8.

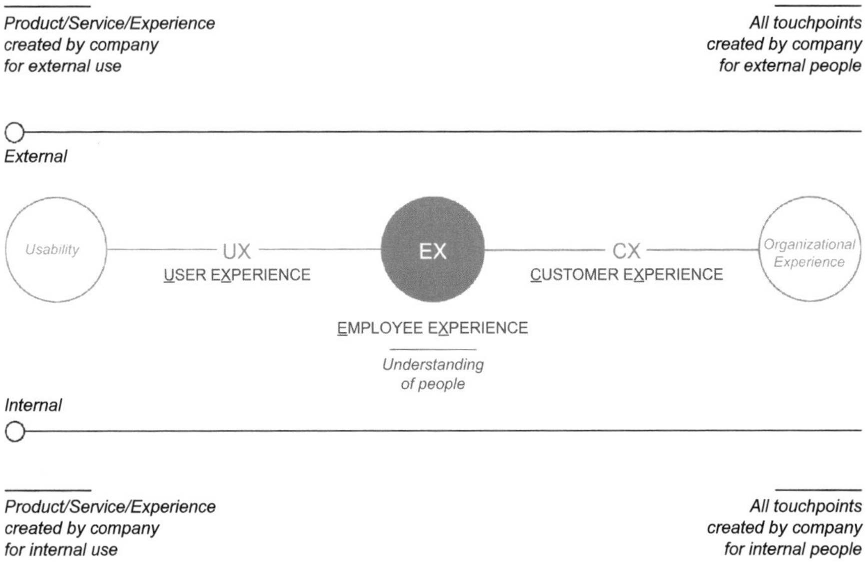
Product/Service/Experience
created by company
for external use
All touchpoints
created by company
for external people
External
Usability
UX
USER EXPERIENCE
EX
EMPLOYEE EXPERIENCE
Understanding
of people
CX
CUSTOMER EXPERIENCE
Organizational
Experience
Internal
Product/Service/Experience
created by company
for internal use
All touchpoints
created by company
for internal people

Fig. 1.8 Definition of Customer Experience

Products (Usability), processes and services (User Experience) as well as all related touch points are customer experience areas that need to be designed efficiently and effectively to achieve customer satisfaction. The crucial touch points (also known as 'moments of truth') have to trigger experiences. For this reason it is also called the customer **experience**. It starts with the right corporate communications and also includes peripheral areas such as the user manual of a screwdriver.

The art of matching the management of these touch points, processes and experiences with the corporate branding and additional measures and controlling is referred to as Customer Experience Management.

Coming from an organizational structure and a holistic point of view, usability constitutes the smallest area and customer experience makes up for the most comprehensive topic (see left-hand chart).

On the operational side, usability is the most complex and largest topic, as all company interfaces have been designed and optimized according to the criteria of efficiency, effectiveness and satisfaction. Customer Experience, on the other hand, means managing all usability and user experience measures within the company (see right-hand chartin Fig. 1.9).

In summary, the areas of the individual topics can be defined as follows:

1.4.1 Usability

Which focuses on:

- Objectivity,
- Instrumental Quality,

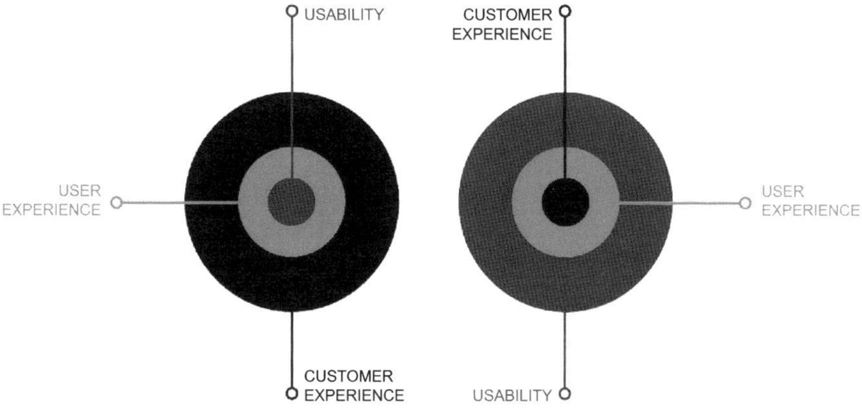
USABILITY
CUSTOMER EXPERIENCE
USER EXPERIENCE
CUSTOMER EXPERIENCE
USER EXPERIENCE
CUSTOMER EXPERIENCE
USABILITY

Fig. 1.9 Usability, User Experience and Customer Experience. Priority Work & Load

- User Tasks,
- Optimized work process design for the product,
- Reduction of Stress,
- Removal of Barriers.

1.4.2 User Experience

Which focuses on:

- Improvement of a product's subjective experience (joy, fun, attractiveness ...)
- Perceived/subjective quality (consequences)
- Developments/trends research
- Challenge and Novelty
- Optimized work process design for products, services, online, as well as offline

1.4.3 Customer Experience

Which focuses on:

- Holistic strategic for all User Experience measures
- Management of all User Experience measures
- Coordination between products, services and branding
- User Experience in Marketing
- Alignment of internal processes
- Controlling of all Experience measures

One keyword that pops up quite frequently within this context is **Design Thinking.**

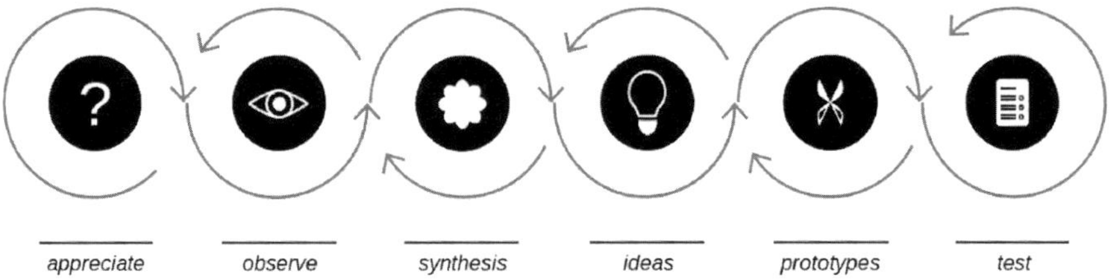
appreciate
observe
synthesis
ideas
prototypes
test

Fig. 1.10 Design Thinking

What is Design Thinking, Fig. 1.10?

Design Thinking refers to an attitude and methodology to develop customer-oriented designs.

As soon as you start to plan a product, or service, you first have to grasp the target, observe the customer, compress the results (synthesis) and use these to develop new ideas and subsequently also iteratively develop and test prototypes.

The elaboration of concepts as well as a product's and services actual design is not part of the basic definition of design thinking. However, this is an essential part in the user experience and the user-centered design process.

What does this really mean for us?

We all are "Design Thinkers", as soon as we integrate the user into the development process and pursue a **Customer-Oriented Process**.

However, this does not yet solve our problem.

- How do I proceed?
- How do I simplify?
- How do I create experiences?

Let's move on to the topics of ease of use and the simplification of products and services.

1.5 Understanding Simplicity

By definition, usability means: "User-friendliness/serviceability"

Serviceability: "*The extent to which a product can be used by specified users within a specified context of use, in order to achieve specified goals in an effective, efficient and satisfying manner*" (DIN EN ISO 9241-110 1998, S. 4).

We refer to the term **Effectiveness** to describe a product or process that enables the achievement of a goal. If a web shop only allows me to view and select products but does not allow me to actually order online the web shop clearly is not effective.

Efficiency describes how well or poorly the goal can be achieved. Thus, it represents the effort the user has to put into achieving his goal. Sticking with the above web shop example, it can be stated that a web shop that requires its customers to walk through a ten-step purchase process while actually only three steps would have to required, showcases an inefficient process. Most likely, a great deal of people will drop out of the laborious purchase process.

Satisfaction is always a subjective state of the end customer. Do you enjoy browsing through a web shop or do you experience a lot of frustration? Satisfaction is a combination of a multitude of properties.

Briefly summarized, it can be stated:

Effective = The target can be reached.
Efficient = The shortest path without any obstacles for the user.
Satisfaction = With a smile.
Usability = Quickly achieving the goal with a smile.

For anyone who determines this concept definition to be too general, there are also precise ISO descriptions available:

EN ISO 9241-110 Dialogue Principles

User interfaces of interactive systems, such as web pages, equipment, or software, should be easily usable.. The part 110 of DIN EN ISO 9241 describes the following principles for the design and evaluation of an interface between an user and a system (dialogue design) and replaces the previous tenth part (ISO 9241-11 2006):

- **Suitability for the task** – suitable functionality, minimization of unnecessary interactions.
- **Self-descriptiveness** – comprehensibility through support/feedback.
- **Suitable for learning** – instructions for the user, using appropriate metaphors, goal: minimal learning time.
- **suitability for individualization** – Adaptability to the user and to his work context.
- **Controllability** – Control of the dialogue by the user.
- **Conformity with user expectations,** – consistency, adaption to the user model.
- **Error tolerance** – Maintaining the operation of the system despite the appearance of unforeseen errors.
- 20130224 – From ISO 9241-11_Requirements for Usability.

Are these principles understandable?

The above constitutes very generic information since there is not one optimal dialogue design for diverse products and services available on the market. There are different requirements, target groups and corporate philosophies. Thus, not all products function in the same way and processes may vary vastly from service to service. However, if the principles of dialogue design are met, the product can be perceived as simple and intuitive.

User-friendliness means the user can apply his personal skills to quickly and easily operate a product, or make use of a service.

If you are a doctor and you quickly understand the hospital software, it is user-friendly. If a mechanic is confronted with the same software, he will probably not find it easily understandable. Still, this does not make the software less intuitive. The mechanic is not the target audience this software was designed for.

Up to this point, I have not yet discovered a single TV instruction manual that was designed in a user-friendly way. Does this make me less intelligent? TVs and their manuals are produced for a very generic target group – the general public. Since we appeal to a broad target audience here, it is much more difficult to write simple instructions or enable an intuitive operation.

A product is user-friendly, when a specific user group can easily comprehend it and operate it intuitively.

As soon as we attempt to design something for a clearly defined target group, we have to pay closer attention to the products or services context. When you construct a racecar for mountain roads you will have to come up with a different design that for a racecar operated on the racetrack – even though the target group will be composed of racers in both cases.

When you design a mobile-based product that shall be used in extreme situations like emergency ambulances you will be confronted with a different context than when you are designing a product for a person who is spending the majority of his day in front of the computer. Thence the context represents an additional requirement for us.

All of these areas need to be taken into consideration when designing a simple product, or service.

Every individual has a different knowledge set and receptiveness levels. Nevertheless, there are various rules that help us with the design of intuitive products as we all share the same basic human requirements. We all have similar traits. Deciphering a binary code will be almost impossible for the large proportion of people. Understanding and interpreting a sunset will be easily feasible for most people. However, the actual understood meanings in this case will most likely vary from person to person.

Especially when it comes to the development of products and processes, usability and user friendliness are often misunderstood.

Usability is not about running quick usability tests and optimizing a product based solely on the results. In order for a product to be user-friendly, many more steps have to be taken. This will typically start with a comprehensive customer analysis and will be comprised of iterative conceptual phases and various testing options. Usability testing is the most common method employed within this context, but it is not the only one.

The subsequent customer-oriented development process in accordance with DIN EN ISO 13407 – Fig. 1.11 – starts with the identification of needs, defines the context of the operation, specifies the product requirements in the next step and then kick off the design. After the evaluation phase the process will continue within either one of the previously mentioned process stages, depending on the outcome of the evaluation. Finally, a product is designed that achieves the predefined goals.

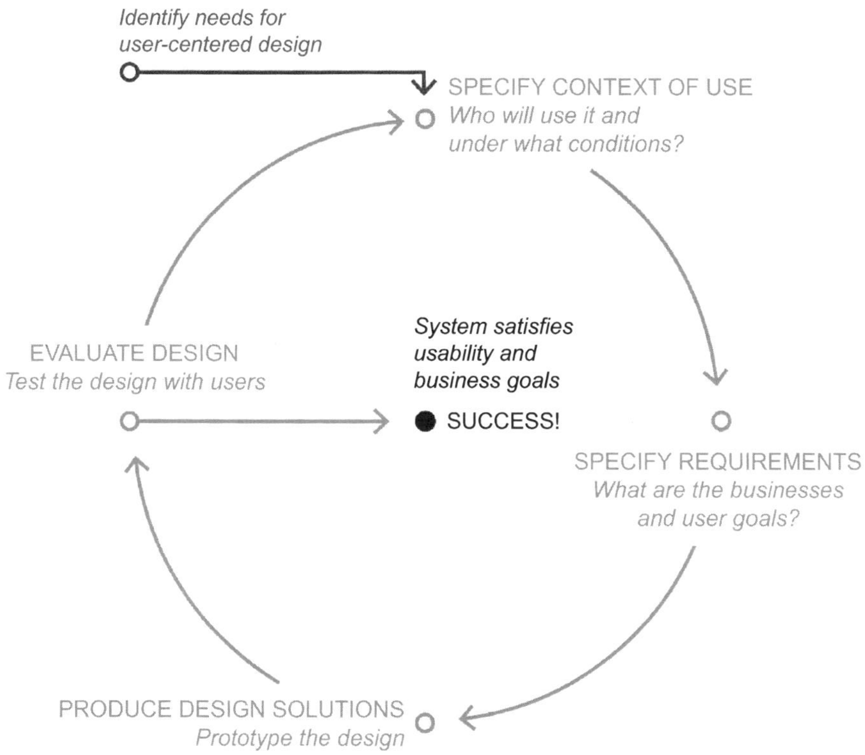
Identify needs for
user-centered design
SPECIFY CONTEXT OF USE
Who will use it and
under what conditions?
System satisfies
usability and
business goals
SUCCESS!
EVALUATE DESIGN
Test the design with users
SPECIFY REQUIREMENTS
What are the businesses
and user goals?
PRODUCE DESIGN SOLUTIONS
Prototype the design

Fig. 1.11 User centered design process

Usability comprises the following criteria:

- Identification and understanding of needs,
- Understanding the steps to be taken,
- Specification of the context of use,
- Specification of customer requirements,
- Production of design solutions,
- Evaluation of designs.

Usability often gets confused with, or wrongly interpreted as the term "usable".

1.6 Usable vs Usability

Example

You are building a house and have it planned by an architect. Of course, you inform him of all the wishes and needs of the entire family, which you have previously obtained. Being the careful person that you are, you state all details and requirements repeatedly to ensure everyone is on the same page.

The architect starts to plan the house, everything seems fine and the actual building begins. After stressful months filled with construction work, your family enters the new dream house for the first time. It does not take long until the first questions come up. Will the children also get a separate bathroom? Where will the closet go? Is this the actual size of the kitchen – it seemed so much bigger on the initial plan? Have you thought about where we can move our fitness equipment?

Were the family's initial desirers and needs not taken seriously? There is no budget for major changes so you try to work with the situation as best as possible. There is no chance of integrating all of these new findings into the plan. After another six months you move in with your family, but you are not happy with the final outcome. Two years later, upon the birth of a new family member, you decide to sell the house and move into a new one. Due to the fact that the needs and wishes were not reviewed and clearly specified in advance, you now have to give up a lot of things.

In fact, in everyday life situations change and new requirements always arise. This holds true for the development of products and services as well. When the end user is integrated too late into the process, or might be confronted with the wrong questions, this can result in large changes that are necessary in final development phases. In this example, when every change costs a fortune in comparison to what it would have cost, we recognize the importance of the right people asking the right questions. When one asks at a late stage, it usually means that only minor changes can be made.

Study
A primary objective of effective usability processes is to accelerate the development time of a software product. A market launch delay of 25 % may result in a revenue loss of up to 50 % (Karat 1994).

Study
The rule of thumb of the Cost-Benefit-Ratio 1-10-100 is still valid today: Once a product is in the implementation phase, the elimination of a problem costs roughly ten times more than in the design phase, Fig. 1.12. If the final product already exists and is being sold, you have to expect that costs will increase a hundredfold (Gilb 2005).

Usability does not revise an almost finished product quickly in order to make it user-friendly before the final launch. Quite often, small changes are only a drop in the bucket. When a basic concept is not fit to the customer, or when core processes are incorrectly defined, all changes are extremely expensive.

At this stage we might succeed in making the product usable however, it will not be user-friendly. Making a product usable requires 20 % effort, while making it user-friendly requires an effort of 80 %, Fig. 1.13. Since a lot more time is invested in user research and iterative developments it is an ideal foundation for innovative and very intuitive products and processes to be created.

As stated, we can make a product usable, but this does simultaneously make the product user-friendly.

► **User-Friendliness Means** Effectively, efficiently and with satisfaction.

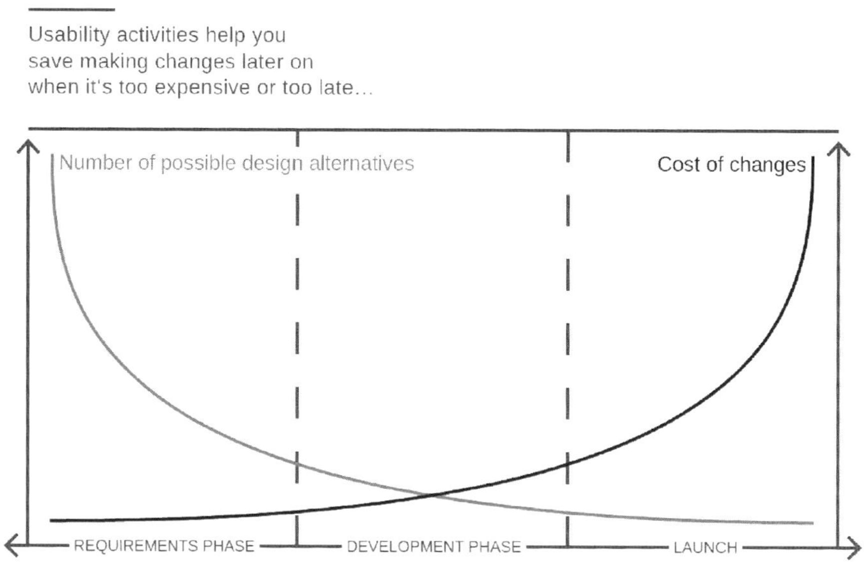
Usability activities help you
save making changes later on
when it's too expensive or too late...
Number of possible design alternatives
Cost of changes
REQUIREMENTS PHASE
DEVELOPMENT PHASE
LAUNCH

Fig. 1.12 Cost-Benefit-Ratio

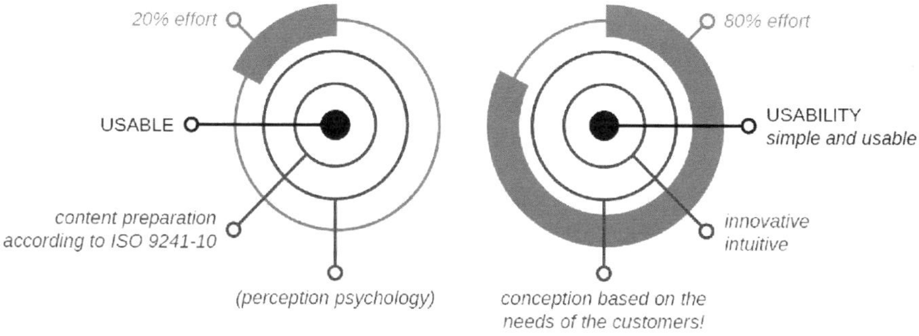
20% effort
USABLE
content preparation
according to ISO 9241-10
(perception psychology)
80% effort
USABILITY
simple and usable
innovative
intuitive
conception based on the
needs of the customers!

Fig. 1.13 Usable versus Usability

Example

In "The Twelve Tasks of Asterix", Asterix and Obelix have to find the permit A38 in "The Place That Sends You Mad". Basically, the organization within the house can be regarded as effective, as there are numerous signs and there appears to always be a clear way to the next office. But would you regard it as an efficient design that satisfies its target audience – Asterix and Obelix – Hardly, Fig. 1.14.

Are you familiar with such situations?

Although the product or service may **somehow** be 'usable', it is anything but user-friendly.

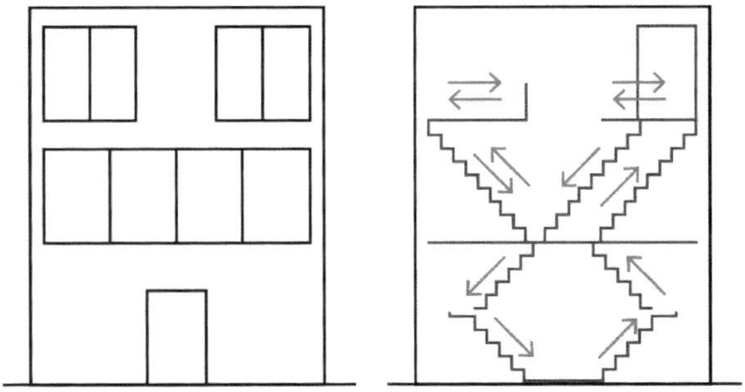

Fig. 1.14 House of insanes

Usability consists of much more than just the visual design of the interface. If you only optimize the visual appearance, the product may be usable, but it is just the tip of the iceberg, Fig. 1.15. To make the product user-friendly, you will need to redesign the entire iceberg, that is to say, the entire system.

The key challenges and efforts are often focused around the optimal design of processes based on the context of use.

When new innovative products are developed, it is paramount to evaluate and conceptualize the context of use in order to place these products successfully in the market, Fig. 1.16.

There are many studies that demonstrate that you need a lot of ideas, but only a small percentage of them are actually being realized and transformed into a suc-

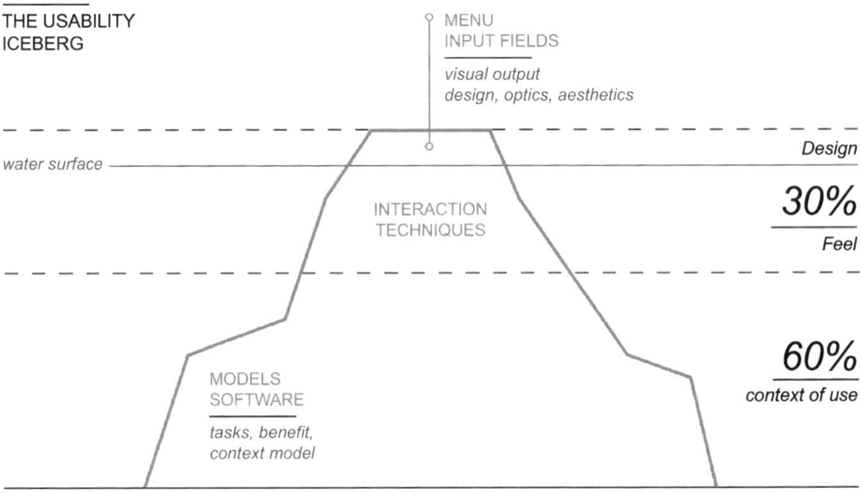
THE USABILITY ICEBERG
MENU
INPUT FIELDS
visual output
design, optics, aesthetics
water surface
Design
30%
Feel
INTERACTION TECHNIQUES
60%
context of use
MODELS
SOFTWARE
tasks, benefit,
context model

Fig. 1.15 Usability Iceberg

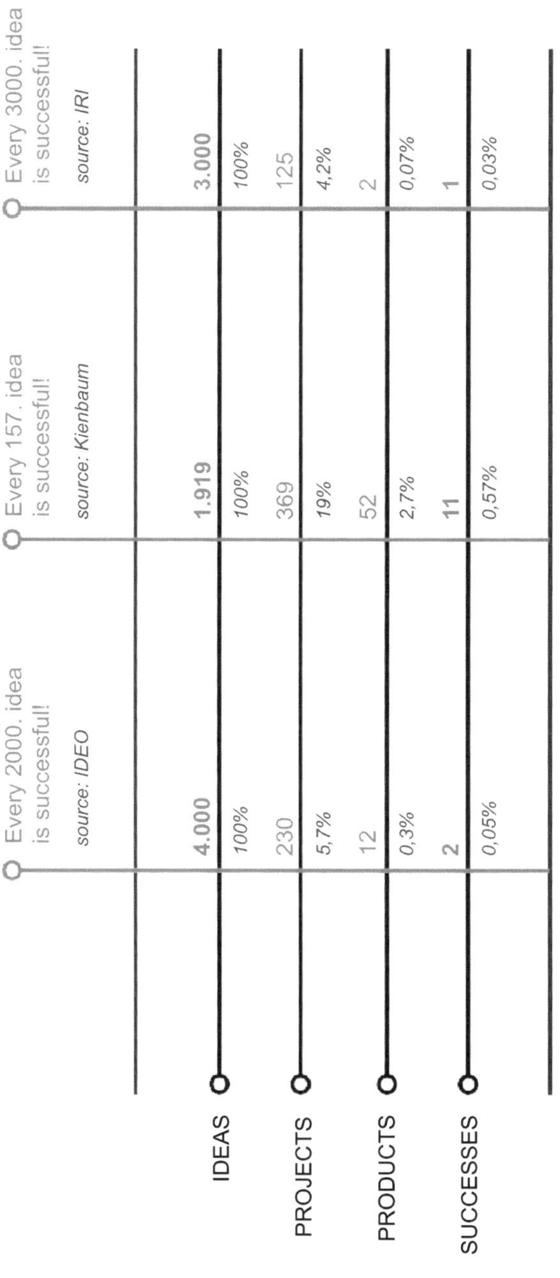
Every 2000. idea
is successful!
source: IDEO
Every 157. idea
is successful!
source: Kienbaum
Every 3000. idea
is successful!
source: IRI
IDEAS
4.000
100%
1.919
100%
3.000
100%
PROJECTS
230
5,7%
369
19%
125
4,2%
PRODUCTS
12
0,3%
52
2,7%
2
0,07%
SUCCESSES
2
0,05%
11
0,57%
1
0,03%

Fig. 1.16 Idea to Product success

cess story. In order to increase this probability a **customer-oriented development process** is indispensable.

Before the actual development of a product or planning of a new service, it is highly recommended to reflect on whether one wishes to create a product that is merely **usable**, or a product that showcases **user-friendliness**.

Once you dispose of a user-friendly, emotional product, you have achieved your objective. From idea to implementation the success rates and the final customer acceptance will be better than the previous.

The following section will provide you with a rough structure of how to kick off the optimal process in order to develop a user-friendly process. After this,

- We will once more review the emotional aspects and will then
- Discuss creative power and innovations.

References

Asterix, © Deutsches Asterix Archiv 1998–2015, Zeichnungen: Albert Uderzo & Didier Conrad – © Les Editions ALBERT-RENÉ, GOSCINNY-UDERZO, Letzte Aktualisierung dieses Eintrages: 5. Mai 2006

DIN EN ISO 9241-110, Ergonomie der Mensch-System-Interaktion (1998)

Gilb: *Gilb, 1988; IBM, 2001; zit. n. Marcus,*(2005)

Heineken, E., & Habermann, T. (1994). *Lernpsychologie für den beruflichen Alltag*. Heidelberg: Sauer.

Herczeg, M. (1994a). *Universität Heidelberg, Software-Ergonomie: Grundlagen der Mensch-Computer-Kommunikation*. Bonn u. a.: Addison-Wesley Verlag. http://www.cl.uni-heidelberg.de/courses/archiv/ws05/mci/MCI-2005-10-25.pdf, Accessed: 01. April 2012

Herczeg, M., & Software-Ergonomie (1994b). *Grundlagen der Mensch-Computer-Kommunikation*. Bonn: Addison-Wesley.

IQew 2006, http://galerie.designnation.de/bild/24845, Accessed 02. January 2015

ISO_9241-11 Die neue DIN EN ISO 9241-110 "Grundsätze der Dialoggestaltung" (01.04.2006)

Karat, C.-M. (1994). A Business Case Approach to UsabilityCost Justification. In R. Bias, & D. Mayhew (Eds.), *Cost-Justifying Usability* (pp. 45–70). New York: Academic Press.

Miller, G. A. (1956). The magical number seven, plus or minus two: Some limits on our capacity for processing information. *Psychological Review*, *63*(2), 81–97.

Preim, B. (1999). *Entwicklung interaktiver Systeme: Grundlagen, Fallbeispiele und innovative Anwendungsfelder*. Taschenbuch. Berlin: Springer.

Scheier, C., & Held, D. (2006). *Wie Werbung wirkt.* München: Haufe Fachbuch.

Siebert, H. (1998). SchulVisionen. In R. Voß (Ed.), *Theorie und Praxis systemisch-konstruktivistischer Pädagogik*. Heidelberg: Carl-Auer-Systeme Verlag.

Schilling (1993). *Dialektik/Methodik des Sozialpädagogik*

Schorpp, R. (2015). Arbeitstechnik Lernen: http://homepage.hispeed.ch/rschorppSeite/Dateien/Lernen_Theorie_V4.pdf, Accessed 12. April 2015

University of California, Berkeley (2003). *How much information?*. http://www.sims.berkeley.edu/research/projects/how-much-info-2003/execsum.htm. Accessed 17. März 2005

2 The Path Towards Simplicity

In the first chapter we learned that the simple processing of information is a fundamental part of the development of an experience. The simplicity of processes and products has an enormous influence on their acceptance by customers and, consequently, on customer satisfaction. In this block you will be reading about rules and ways in which you can prepare information simply for your target group. You will learn the path to simplicity, from broad-brush approaches all the way through to clear instructions. A presentation of various methods from usability and user experience will give you an insight into the way you should work.

In order for a product or service to be perceived as intuitive and simple it has to be either:

- Efficient and effective so no user hurdles can occur

or, when it comes to very complex systems:

- The overall system must be recognizable and the processes have to be consistently depicted in order for the user to follow the plan and never lose his point of reference.

This applies to any kind of complexity. Within the first step of any redesign or development the problem solution must be in the foreground. The rkww principle may be of help:

R → Really
K → Know
W → What
W → Want

The core idea of all products and services always lies in the actual problem solution or in the satisfaction of a need. Thus, products and services are set up to make something better, faster, desirable, easier, or more enjoyable.

J. Robier, *UX Redefined*, Management for Professionals, DOI 10.1007/978-3-319-21062-9_2

From a customer perspective, this basic task should be designed as easily and intuitively as possible. Then, when the basic problem is solved and the basic need is met, it is possible to offer the user a new range of add-on options. However they must never dilute the core task.

- The core task of a hair dryer is to dry hair.
- An electrician has the core task of ensuing a flowing current.
- A hotel has to answer the need for shelter, safety and ultimately a temporary replacement for one's home.

When you want to simplify your service or product, look for its core idea, the added value and the actual reason for a customers desire to buy. This process has to be easily visible and comprehensible for the customer.

► In general complexity follows over time in the form of further developments that accommodate additional customer needs. Nevertheless, it is important to find the heartbeat of your product.

Your product or service should solve no more than **three** needs. When more needs are met, it can be assumed that the product or service in question is diluted and can be simplified again.

2.1 Find Your Heartbeat

When we attempt to simplify a system it is paramount to reduce the product's information overload. To be optimized for human perception the product needs to be reduced to its very core. However, this does not imply that all existing functionalities or services need to be deleted.

The left image illustrates a system with a multitude of features that are not linked to the product's core, Fig. 2.1. In contrast, the right image system encompasses a lot of information (features, services) that is closely connected with the core and is branched out. The heart represents the reason for a customer to buy the product. Through additional information it may be upgraded and refined – or it might as well become less clear and more complex as showcased in the left image.

Between a gem and lots of pebbles often lies only a stones width.

The heart of a coffee machine is to brew coffee. The additional underlying need is typically an energy boost. Thus, this boost has to be achieved in the fastest and easiest way possible.

Looking at the process of buying a new coffee machine, it can be stated that the machine can have many functionalities, but the key objective, the heartbeat, is a cup of coffee. Consequently, the process of opening the packaging to actually being able to drink the first cup of coffee has to be as lean and simple as possible.

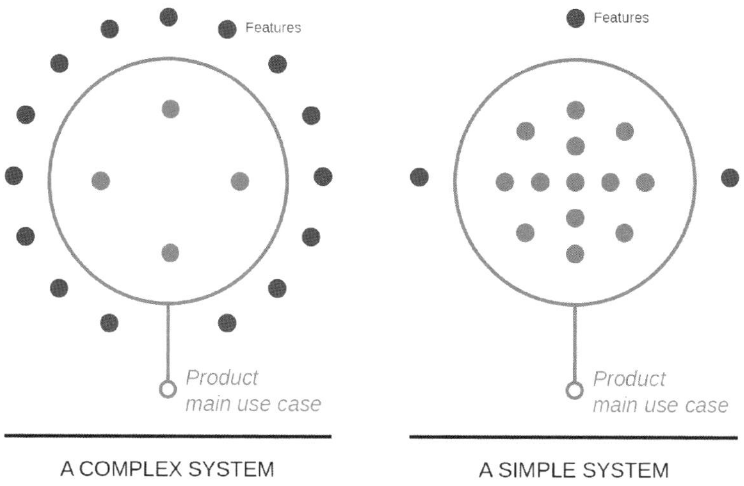
Features
Product
main use case
A COMPLEX SYSTEM
Features
Product
main use case
A SIMPLE SYSTEM

Fig. 2.1 Complex system versus easy system

1. Open the pack.
2. Plug in and switch on the coffee machine.
3. Fill in water.
4. Fill in coffee beans.
5. Coffee preparation.
6. Drink the coffee.

This represents the shortest way to get a cup of coffee. Once the coffee machine is then set up it must be just as easy to continue to use it.

1. Coffee preparation.
2. Drink coffee.

If special features are available, such as altering the dosage of the coffee strength, the cup size, the functionality does not necessarily have to be as easy. Clearly, this would be desirable, but if the additional functionalities take a little longer, it is not a big issue since they represent an added value for the user. Nevertheless, the core process must remain simple.

Let's discuss another simple example: online search engines. In the beginning every search engine had numerous features and additional information on its website. Then one search engine appeared that took the market by storm.

Google was the first search engine that was reduced to its very heartbeat

2008: Fig. 2.2.
2013: Fig. 2.3.

The main functionality is the actual search and this is exactly where Google put its focus by only offering one input field. There are no preferences or pre-selections that have to be set. There is only one search box and all additional information and

Web Bilder Maps News Shopping E-Mail Mehr ▾
iGoogle | Anmelden
Google™
Deutschland
Erweiterte Suche
Einstellungen
Sprachtools
Google-Suche
Auf gut Glück!
Suche: Das Web Seiten auf Deutsch Seiten aus Deutschland
Werben mit Google - Unternehmensangebote - Über Google - Google.com in English
©2008 - Datenschutz

Fig. 2.2 Google Start Page (source: Google 2008)

Google
Österreich
Google-Suche
Auf gut Glück!
Neu! Suchergebnisse gibt es jetzt auch mit Geruch - Google Nose ausprobieren

Fig. 2.3 Google Start Page (source: Google 2013)

functionalities are presented in a tiny form in the upper frame. Google's success proves this concept's power and potential impact, Fig. 2.4.

However, Google works on further reduction. Have a look at the main landing page in Fig. 2.5 in January 2015.

The heart remains the search and this is being prioritized above everything else. The main functionalities are displayed through direct access while additional features are hidden behind an icon, Fig. 2.6.

+Hannes Suche Bilder Maps Play YouTube News Gmail Drive Kalender Mehr
Google
Österreich
Google-Suche
Auf gut Glück!

Fig. 2.4 Google Start Page (source: Google 2013)

+Hannes
Gmail
Bilder
Google
Österreich
Google-Suche
Auf gut Glück!

Fig. 2.5 Google Start Page (source: Google 2015)

Fig. 2.6 Google App Icon

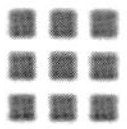

Now, let's take a closer look at another renowned example that has caused quite a stir. Amazon specializes in shopping and therefore has reduced its entire purchase process to one click. The heart of Amazon is process of searching and finding of relevant products. The "One Click Shopping Button" reduced the entire purchase process to one single click. **Amazon specialized itself on its heartbeat**, Fig. 2.7.

Every product and service has to fulfill a primary task that constitutes the reason for its creation and design. This core element, this heartbeat, in the first stages this is where the focus has to be set.

In order to find innovative, new, or intuitive approaches, applying the methodology of sceneries is highly recommended.

To put this into practice, trying to adopt your customer's point of view as soon as you have found your heartbeat is ideal. Slowly walk through the entire process once more without paying attention to technical, structural or organizational requirements. In usability, this method is also known as the 'Cognitive Walkthrough'.

What does the process of my product have to look like in order to enable the customer to attain his goal in the fastest and easiest fashion?

Ask yourself the following questions:

- What is the heart that drives your system?
- Is it in the foreground?
- Is the main process established with clarity and simplicity?
- Can you reach the goal as efficiently as possible?
- How long does it take you to do so?
- Do you get distracted?

As soon as you have resolved these questions you must attempt to determine your system's target audience and define it as precisely as possible.

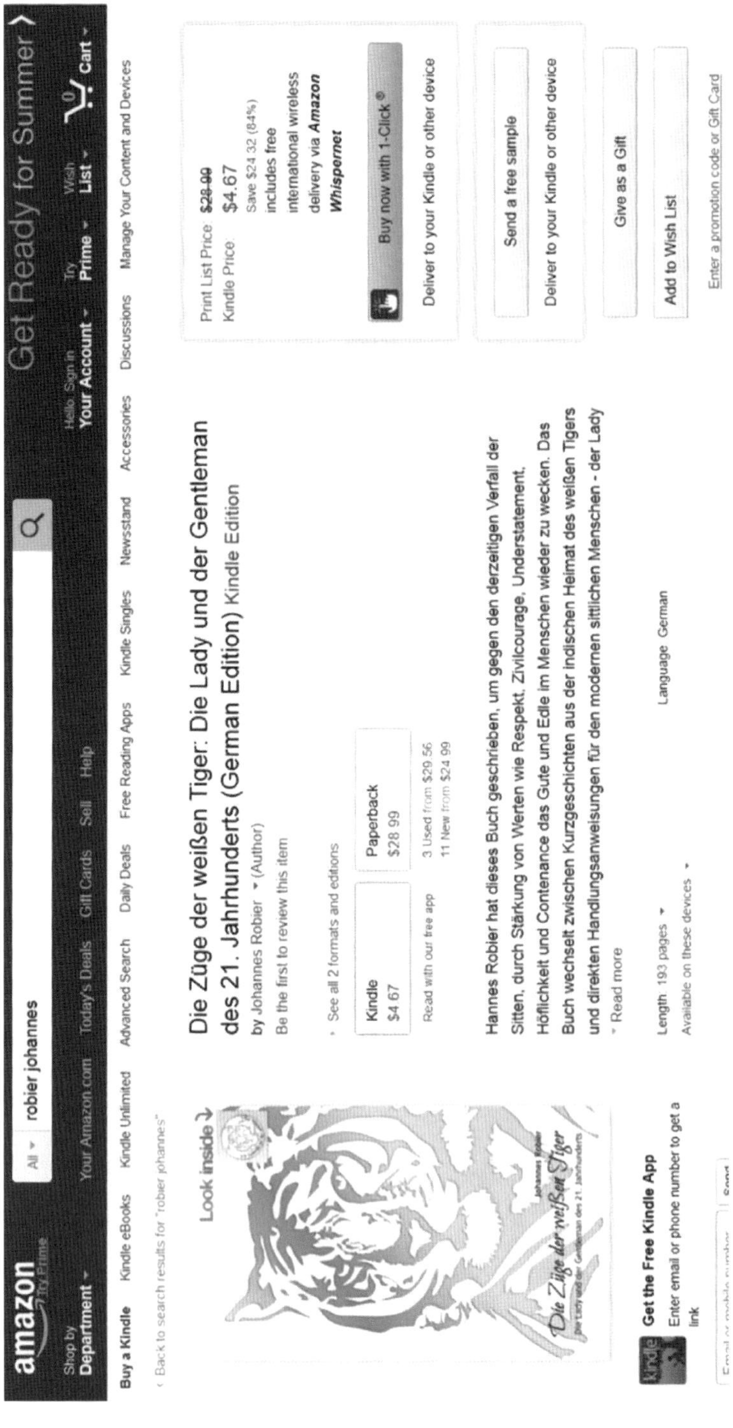
amazon
Try Prime
Shop by Department
All
robier johannes
Your Amazon.com
Today's Deals
Gift Cards
Sell
Help
Get Ready for Summer
Hello. Sign in
Your Account
Try Prime
Wish List
Cart
Buy a Kindle
Kindle eBooks
Kindle Unlimited
Advanced Search
Daily Deals
Free Reading Apps
Kindle Singles
Newsstand
Accessories
Discussions
Manage Your Content and Devices
Back to search results for "robier johannes"
Look inside
Die Züge der weißen Tiger: Die Lady und der Gentleman des 21. Jahrhunderts (German Edition) Kindle Edition
by Johannes Robier (Author)
Be the first to review this item
See all 2 formats and editions
Kindle $4.67
Paperback $28.99
Read with our free app
3 Used from $29.56
11 New from $24.99
Hannes Robier hat dieses Buch geschrieben, um gegen den derzeitigen Verfall der Sitten, durch Stärkung von Werten wie Respekt, Zivilcourage, Understatement, Höflichkeit und Contenance das Gute und Edle im Menschen wieder zu wecken. Das Buch wechselt zwischen Kurzgeschichten aus der indischen Heimat des weißen Tigers und direkten Handlungsanweisungen für den modernen sittlichen Menschen - der Lady
Read more
Length: 193 pages
Language: German
Available on these devices
Print List Price: $28.99
Kindle Price: $4.67
Save $24.32 (84%)
includes free international wireless delivery via Amazon Whispernet
Buy now with 1-Click®
Deliver to your Kindle or other device
Send a free sample
Deliver to your Kindle or other device
Give as a Gift
Add to Wish List
Enter a promotion code or Gift Card
Get the Free Kindle App
Enter email or phone number to get a link
Send

Fig. 2.7 Example of a product page (source: Amazon 2015)

2.2 What are Your "Personas"?

At the next stage a separation into different target groups needs to happen before the product can move on into the conceptual phase. One could assume that global corporations with global products and a global target group do not work with specific target groups and do not differentiate between workers, managers, students, or seniors. In fact, they have to narrowly define their target audiences as well and differentiate their products accordingly. Of course, they need to design their products as simply and intuitively as possible in order for the majority of the population to adopt it. Nevertheless, adjustments are typically indispensable and happen on a regional basis.

Specific products or services that have specific target audiences such as doctors, lawyers, or engineers, need to be aligned with their user groups. It could be possible that initial customers who make the purchase decision will not be the end-users in this case. Thus, executives may be the ones who need to be convinced of the product in an initial stage however, the end-users will have to be won over afterwards.

Example

As an example, let's discuss the check-in process at airports. The target group is being separated according to the amount of money spent – First Class, Business Class and Economy Class. Hence, if an airline decided to have all its first-class customers check in along with the ones from the other classes the added value would be lost. Consequently the target audience would be very likely to either pay less or grow smaller.

This means products should be classified in such a manner that allows for processes to be developed as efficiently as possible based on its respective target group.

Another typical separation in this context is the target audience split up into first users and heavy users. There are groups of people who will only use a product occasionally and other groups that will do so quite often, if not everyday. These target groups have diverse needs and approaches to use a product or service.

In order to dive into a first evaluation phase and determine the target audience, consider the stakeholder map in Fig. 2.8 and note all individuals who will be responsible for, or touched by the project. Do not skip any group of people.

Enter all users who have influence on your system from top to bottom and those who use the system from left to right, based on the frequency of usage.

Your target audiences can now be found in the left area. Based on this, you can find your primary target audience which should consists of those people who

- Use the system with the highest frequency,
- Generate the most revenue,
- Are the most experienced,
- Take the most influence.

Based on the above, you are able to define the main target group.

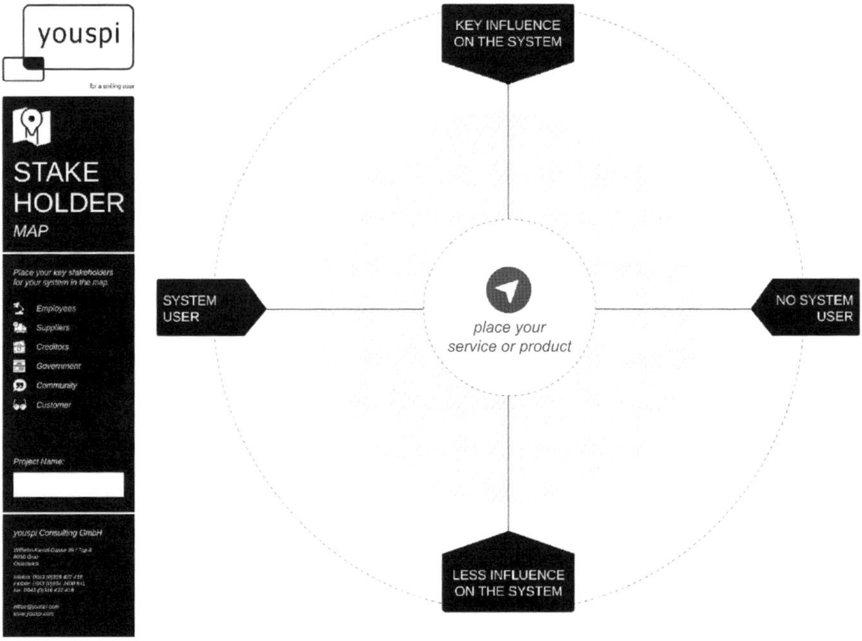
youspi
STAKE HOLDER MAP
Place your key stakeholders for your system in the map.
Employees
Suppliers
Creditors
Government
Community
Customer
Project Name:
youspi Consulting GmbH
KEY INFLUENCE ON THE SYSTEM
SYSTEM USER
place your service or product
NO SYSTEM USER
LESS INFLUENCE ON THE SYSTEM

Fig. 2.8 Stakeholder Map

In addition to the main target group, the next two most important target audiences have to be defined in a next step, along with a proper definition of your NONE-target groups. This will ensure that the actual future users and non-users will be kept in mind of developers and designers throughout the entire project.

Once these target groups have been defined, the next step is to find out more about their needs and behaviors. The following methods are often employed to point these out:

- Ethnographic Studies,
- Interviews,
- In-Depth Interviews,
- Observations,
- A Day in the life of,
- Shadowing.

In order to specify the target groups, their respective needs and to structure these findings properly, the methodology of needs setting evaluation can help.

For each identified area, please note all applicable needs, Fig. 2.9. Then, move on to eliciting the ten most important ones and write them in the bottom boxes, along with short notes.

The best and easiest way to make the target groups visible for a development team or an entire organization is the concept of Personas.

Personas represent a user experience methodology that enables the depiction of the target group as a "typical person."

It is constructed as follows in Fig. 2.10.

Personas help us in the development of services and products to better understand the target group. Through observations and interviews need-based target groups are defined – Personas. The findings are then depicted in a pictorial form which allows for a better identification with the target group and enables the project team to put itself in their target group's position.

Personas are created with a picture, a name, typical characteristics and hobbies. Their mentality is typically depicted in a rather exaggerated way, as this allows to also cover the average user. A persona always contains a description of his or her requirement for the actual product, whereby no solutions are described – only emotional demands.

A student once walked up to me and said, "For the first time ever, we created personas in a project and presented those, along with the copywriting, to the graphic designer. Looking at these, he then stated that this was the first time for him to actually realize whom he was designing for and that this made his work a lot easier."

Personas enable all project participants to get a clearer and more distinct idea of the target group. This entails not only the fact that the product gets simpler, but even that the communication within the team is facilitated as a common view is defined.

Create personas upon every project's kick-off and make sure that they are kept alive during the various project phases. In this context, it is paramount to note that personas should never be based on your point of view only – rather, they should be a representation of the results of a qualitative analysis. This will help tremendously in creating sustainable and successful products.

As soon as you have defined and developed your personas and also your non-personas, you can move on to create a contextual map, Fig. 2.11.

The contextual map shows in which areas of life and in which surroundings the work will get done. External influences are also included in this chart and it is important to note for example, whether the work will be done during the day or night and whether it will be cold or hot.

Do you expect to find yourself in a stressful situation during the project execution, or will there be enough time?

Complete the contextual map as this will help you set the right priorities within the next phase. When the design phase starts, the better and more detailed you have worked up to this point, the easier will this next phase be.

Example

In order to better illustrate the use of personas and the contextual map, consider the development of a controller for a biomass heating system. The four main target groups are defined as follows:

- Homeowners who renew their heating system (50+),
- People who construct their own houses (Alter 20–40),
- Heating System Distributors,
- Service staff (repairs).

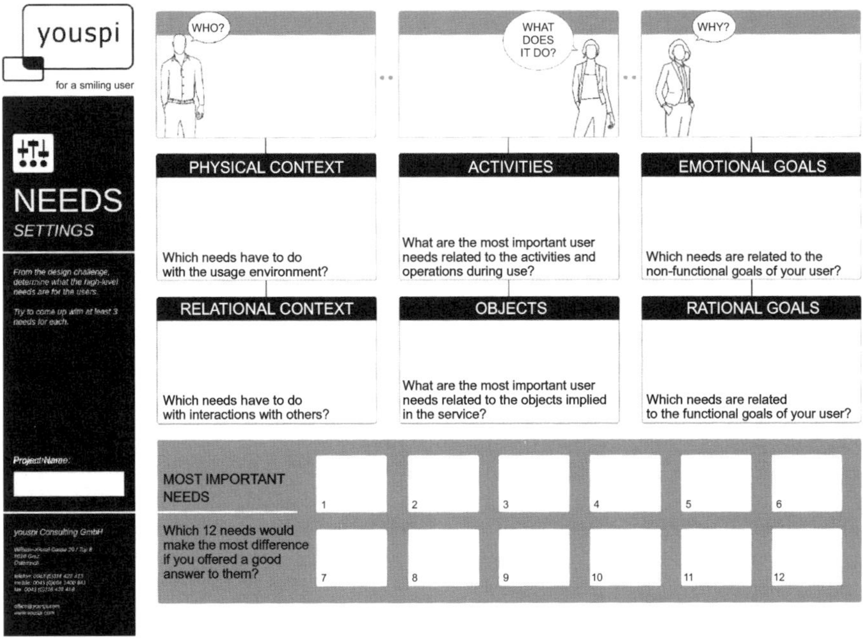
youspi
for a smiling user
NEEDS
SETTINGS
From the design challenge, determine what the high-level needs are for the users.
Try to come up with at least 3 needs for each.
Project Name:
youspi Consulting GmbH
WHO?
WHAT DOES IT DO?
WHY?
PHYSICAL CONTEXT
Which needs have to do with the usage environment?
ACTIVITIES
What are the most important user needs related to the activities and operations during use?
EMOTIONAL GOALS
Which needs are related to the non-functional goals of your user?
RELATIONAL CONTEXT
Which needs have to do with interactions with others?
OBJECTS
What are the most important user needs related to the objects implied in the service?
RATIONAL GOALS
Which needs are related to the functional goals of your user?
MOST IMPORTANT NEEDS
Which 12 needs would make the most difference if you offered a good answer to them?
1
2
3
4
5
6
7
8
9
10
11
12

Fig. 2.9 Needs Settings

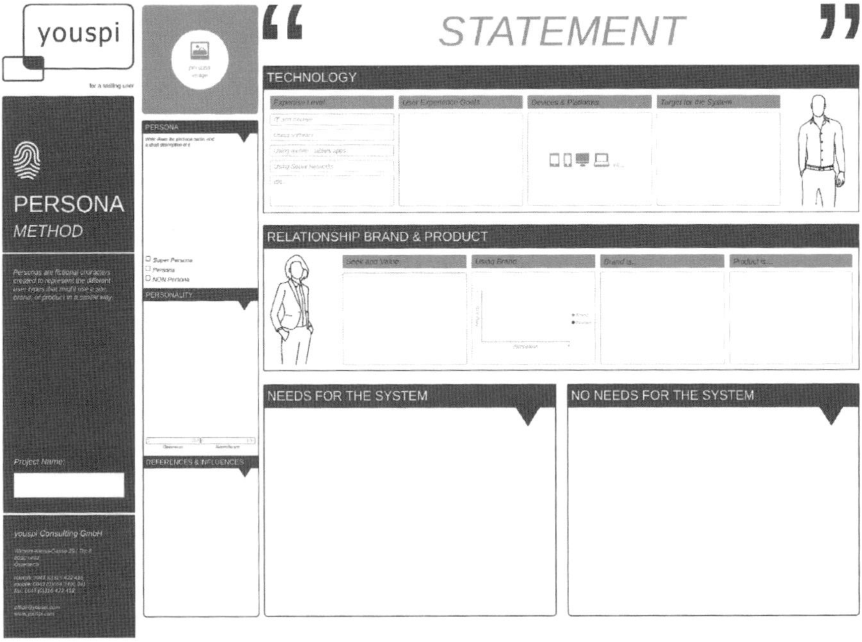
youspi
PERSONA
METHOD
Project Name:
youspi Consulting GmbH
PERSONA
PERSONALITY
REFERENCES & INFLUENCES
STATEMENT
TECHNOLOGY
RELATIONSHIP BRAND & PRODUCT
NEEDS FOR THE SYSTEM
NO NEEDS FOR THE SYSTEM

Fig. 2.10 Persona method

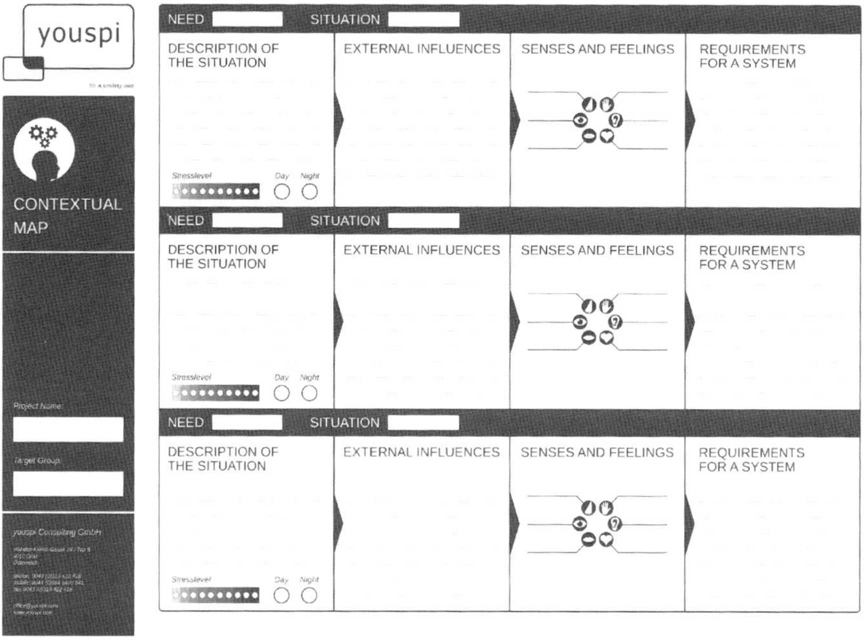
youspi
CONTEXTUAL MAP
Project Name:
Target Group:
youspi Consulting GmbH
NEED
SITUATION
DESCRIPTION OF THE SITUATION
EXTERNAL INFLUENCES
SENSES AND FEELINGS
REQUIREMENTS FOR A SYSTEM
Stresslevel
Day
Night

Fig. 2.11 Contextual Map

If you start to define these in greater detail you realize that they all have their own features and work within specific contexts. The first two groups want to be able to operate the heating system, while the distributors and service staff have to be able to work efficiently with it and want no chances to the existing controller.

Rough definition of groups 1 + 2:

- Maximum of 6 main functionalities,
- Operation in the basement or via a remote control,
- No time pressure to operate the system,
- Rare access to the control system.

Rough definition of groups 3 + 4:

- More than 50 functions for calibration and adjustments,
- Operation control happens on the device itself,
- Time pressure to operate the system,
- Daily access, efficiency is paramount.

Clearly, it was a challenge to unify both groups into one interaction concept. In the following picture you can see that the left side was designed with large icons for the end customer, while a list view was integrated on the right side for efficient use for professionals. The old control remained the same, Fig. 2.12.

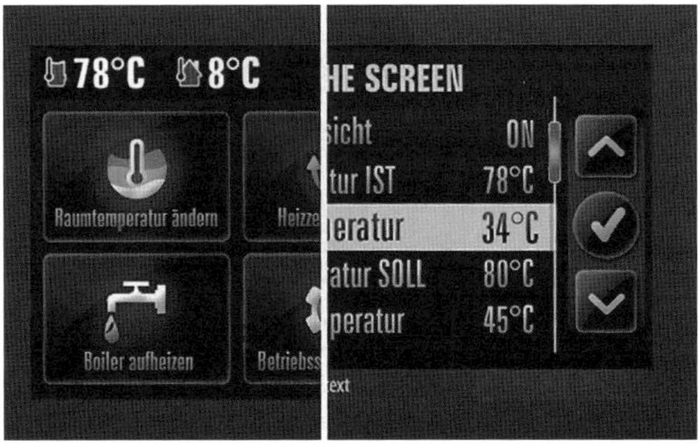
78°C 8°C
HE SCREEN
icht ON
tur IST 78°C
eratur 34°C
atur SOLL 80°C
peratur 45°C
Raumtemperatur ändern
Boiler aufheizen

Fig. 2.12 KWB control – Graphical Interface by youspi

We will come back to this example from KWB at a later point when we dive into the areas of holistic design and innovation.

2.3 Prioritization Increases Your Return on Investment!

Each product and every information process thrives on prioritization. Furthermore, the human perception has put its focus on the prioritization of information, underlying its importance.

Our body's physical condition requires us to prioritize. Out of the 30–100 million bit/s of available information, we can only consciously perceive 100 bit/s, Fig. 2.13. To emphasize this we need to consider a renowned example which illustrates our

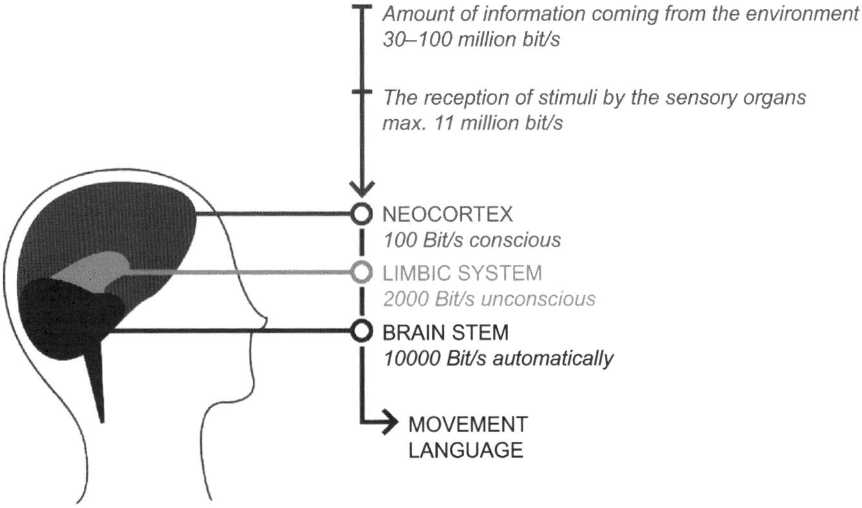
Amount of information coming from the environment
30–100 million bit/s
The reception of stimuli by the sensory organs
max. 11 million bit/s
NEOCORTEX
100 Bit/s conscious
LIMBIC SYSTEM
2000 Bit/s unconscious
BRAIN STEM
10000 Bit/s automatically
MOVEMENT
LANGUAGE

Fig. 2.13 Human Information recording – Compare KH Pflug brain's performance and ways of functioning which proves that our reading habits do not change as long as the initial and last letter of the word remains the same.

> The brain poririzeptis the most ipmanortt lrtetes and caerets the raimnenig stenence besad on waht is arleday kwnon.

The brain prioritizes the most important letters and creates the remaining sentence based on what is already known (Rawlinson 1976).

For the processing of information, this means that you need to set anchor points throughout entire interaction processes in order for your brain to stay focused and work with the information properly. In the absence of such anchor points, obstacles and operating errors are inevitable.

Thus there is also no point in presenting important information on an equal level with other functionalities. Let's have a look at another example:

Example

Please select the most important word below:

stone the hill house pine word beer most important baby gorilla hole two small stuff usability sample interaction design vibrant yes human word child color game meal purchase decision is counterpoint pretty return on investment prioritization world actor experience

Were you able to select the right word? No? Actually, it is not feasible because all the words are prioritized on an equal level. When all words are prioritized on an equal level in an interaction it is not possible to reach the goal.

How about the next example?

stone **the** hill house pine word beer **most important** baby gorilla hole two small stuff usability sample interaction design vibrant yes human **word** child color game meal purchase decision **is** counterpoint pretty return on investment **prioritization** world actor experience

Clearly, this makes the task easier, since an entire combination of words was highlighted and was thereby put into context. However, the word we are looking for could still be any of the six highlighted words as there is not distinction among them.

stone **the** hill house pine word beer **most important**

baby gorilla hole two small stuff usability sample

interaction design vibrant yes human **word** child

color game meal purchase decision **is** counterpoint

pretty return on investment **prioritization** world

actor experience

Highlighting allows you to set graphic accents. An additional prioritization, such as altering the size of elements makes the filtering of information even easier and allows one to quickly grasp information to be focused on – and which information can be skipped. Additional grouping of information further facilitates the interpretation.

the most important word is

prioritization

stone hill house pine word beer baby gorilla hole two small stuff usability sample interaction design vibrant yes human child color game meal purchase decision counterpoint pretty return on investment world actor experience

If the goal was now to make one word stand out even more and be noted as the most important one, a product developer could also hide all other words making the one word an entire new product. Then the only word left is:

prioritization

In contrast to the first example, it is very easy to understand. In order to design in a clear and comprehensible pattern these prioritization steps should be incorporated into every development of products, services and processes. Let's review the presented ways of displaying information:

- Prioritization through color and size,
- Grouping,
- Omitting or hiding information.

Microsoft Word is a good example for periodization and grouping, Fig. 2.14. How can a form be simplified?

The first graph was the starting point of a new concept, Fig. 2.15.

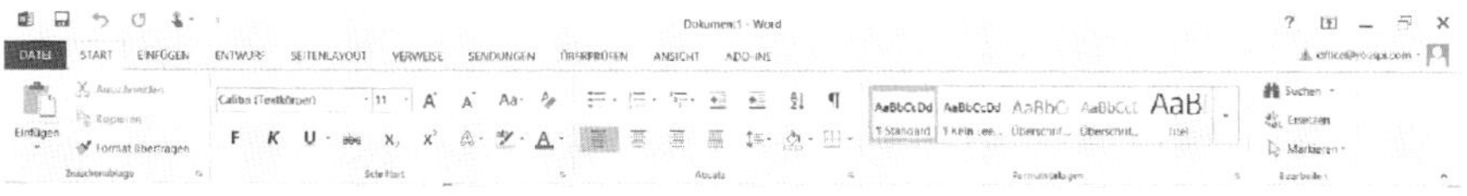
DATEI
START
EINFÜGEN
ENTWURF
SEITENLAYOUT
VERWEISE
SENDUNGEN
ÜBERPRÜFEN
ANSICHT
ADD-INS
Einfügen
AaBbCcDd
AaBbCcDd
AaBb

Fig. 2.14 Prioritization and grouping of functions

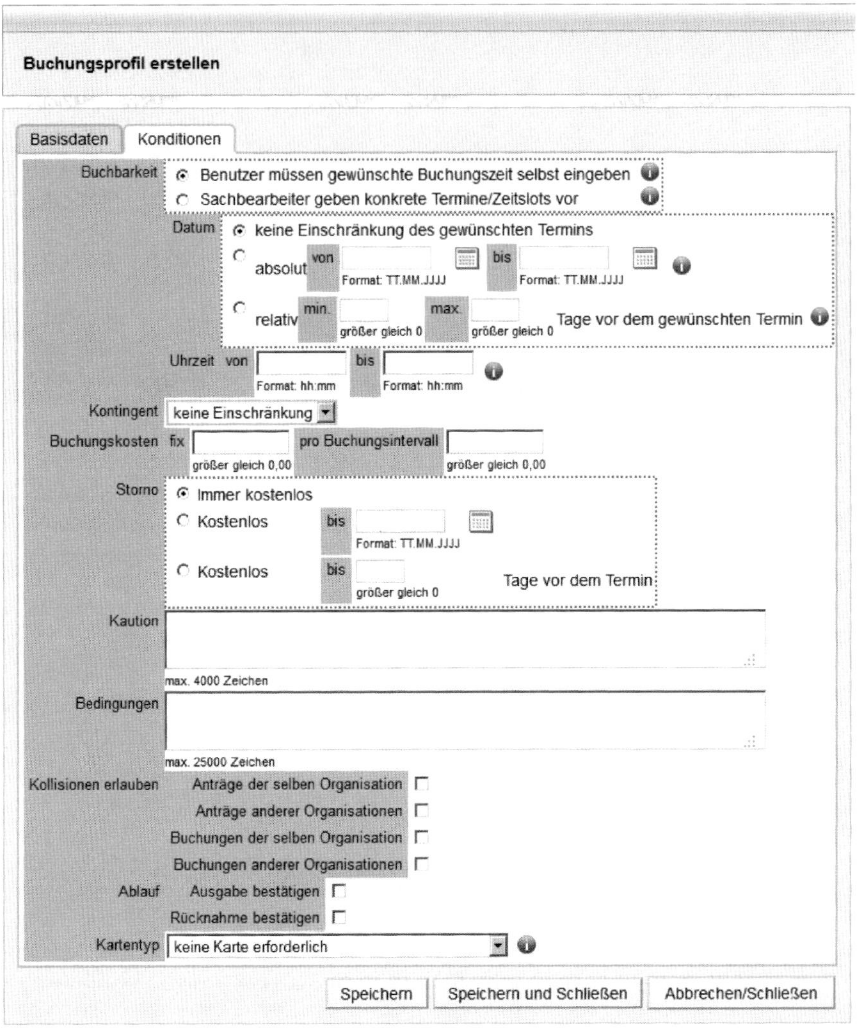
Buchungsprofil erstellen
Basisdaten
Konditionen
Buchbarkeit
Benutzer müssen gewünschte Buchungszeit selbst eingeben
Sachbearbeiter geben konkrete Termine/Zeitslots vor
Datum
keine Einschränkung des gewünschten Termins
absolut
von
Format: TT.MM.JJJJ
bis
Format: TT.MM.JJJJ
relativ
min.
größer gleich 0
max.
größer gleich 0
Tage vor dem gewünschten Termin
Uhrzeit von
Format: hh:mm
bis
Format: hh:mm
Kontingent
keine Einschränkung
Buchungskosten fix
größer gleich 0,00
pro Buchungsintervall
größer gleich 0,00
Storno
Immer kostenlos
Kostenlos
bis
Format: TT.MM.JJJJ
Kostenlos
bis
größer gleich 0
Tage vor dem Termin
Kaution
max. 4000 Zeichen
Bedingungen
max. 25000 Zeichen
Kollisionen erlauben
Anträge der selben Organisation
Anträge anderer Organisationen
Buchungen der selben Organisation
Buchungen anderer Organisationen
Ablauf
Ausgabe bestätigen
Rücknahme bestätigen
Kartentyp
keine Karte erforderlich
Speichern
Speichern und Schließen
Abbrechen/Schließen

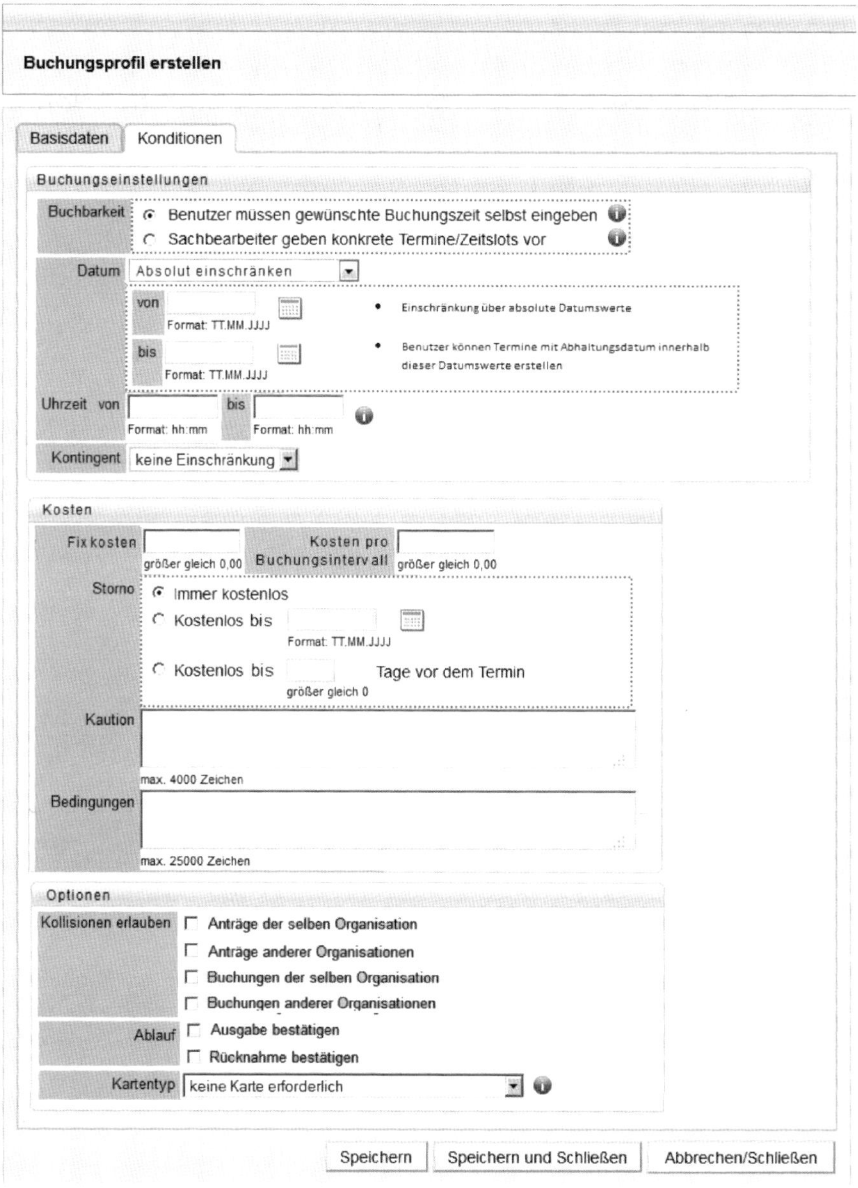
Buchungsprofil erstellen
Basisdaten
Konditionen
Buchungseinstellungen
Buchbarkeit
Benutzer müssen gewünschte Buchungszeit selbst eingeben
Sachbearbeiter geben konkrete Termine/Zeitslots vor
Datum
Absolut einschränken
von
Format: TT.MM.JJJJ
bis
Format: TT.MM.JJJJ
Einschränkung über absolute Datumswerte
Benutzer können Termine mit Abhaltungsdatum innerhalb dieser Datumswerte erstellen
Uhrzeit von
Format: hh:mm
bis
Format: hh:mm
Kontingent
keine Einschränkung
Kosten
Fixkosten
größer gleich 0,00
Kosten pro Buchungsintervall
größer gleich 0,00
Storno
Immer kostenlos
Kostenlos bis
Format: TT.MM.JJJJ
Kostenlos bis
Tage vor dem Termin
größer gleich 0
Kaution
max. 4000 Zeichen
Bedingungen
max. 25000 Zeichen
Optionen
Kollisionen erlauben
Anträge der selben Organisation
Anträge anderer Organisationen
Buchungen der selben Organisation
Buchungen anderer Organisationen
Ablauf
Ausgabe bestätigen
Rücknahme bestätigen
Kartentyp
keine Karte erforderlich
Speichern
Speichern und Schließen
Abbrechen/Schließen

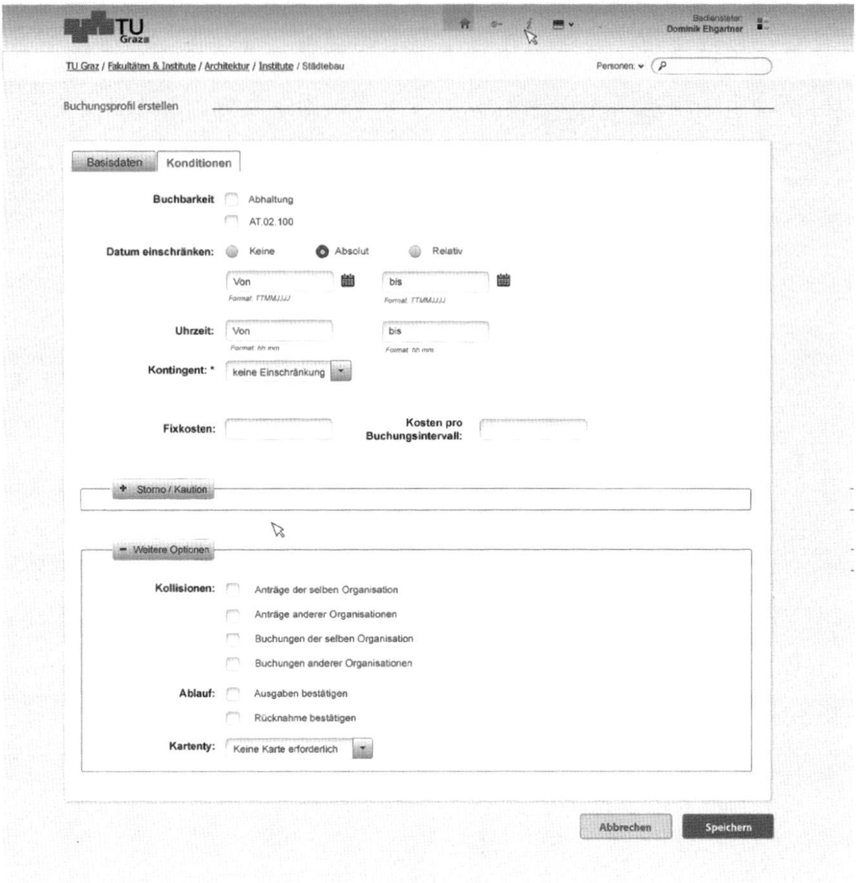
TU Graz
TU Graz / Fakultäten & Institute / Architektur / Institute / Städtebau
Personen
Buchungsprofil erstellen
Basisdaten
Konditionen
Buchbarkeit
Abhaltung
AT.02.100
Datum einschränken:
Keine
Absolut
Relativ
Von
bis
Uhrzeit:
Von
bis
Kontingent: *
keine Einschränkung
Fixkosten:
Kosten pro Buchungsintervall:
Storno / Kaution
Weitere Optionen
Kollisionen:
Anträge der selben Organisation
Anträge anderer Organisationen
Buchungen der selben Organisation
Buchungen anderer Organisationen
Ablauf:
Ausgaben bestätigen
Rücknahme bestätigen
Kartenty:
Keine Karte erforderlich
Abbrechen
Speichern

Fig. 2.15 Form Design in three steps (source: CAMPUSonline)

The second graph was redesigned ‘in-house’.

The third graph however, was defined according to all the rules but without a user analysis. The difference is quickly visible and through a user analysis this graph could be optimized even more.

The three presented simplification options can help achieve a great deal. It is essential to apply the following methods:

1. Heartbeat,
2. Personas,
3. Contextual Inquiries,
4. Prioritization.

This prioritization must be designed in a holistic manner, from the basic problem definition down to the last detail. Thus, processes become clear and visible to the audience.

Through sustainable optimization measures and a clear depiction of the problem solution, it is possible to reduce process duration from two days to two hours or to achieve major sales increases. However, these are only a few of the possible effects that can easily be reached in your organization when you begin to apply these methods and principles. The prioritization of processes can result in a significant business success.

Based on this we can move on to the stage of simplification: Maintaining a consistent design.

2.4 Consistency is the Key for Success

Regardless of how simple, extensive, complicated or intuitive your product is: once you have introduced a certain behavior, you have to keep this consistent over time. People become quickly accustomed to products and behaviors and if these are inconsistent the users are easily dissatisfied and irritated. In turn, service calls are inevitable.

Designing something in a consistent way is quite a challenge given the variety of devices and user requirements on the market. How can you move forward when you wish to offer a solution that must work on Windows Phone, Desktop, iOs, Android, diverse tablets and the web, not to mention the offline world?

Pushing the same interaction concept through all interfaces would clearly be the wrong approach within this example. No user will be in touch with all of the mentioned devices. Typically, a user will work with one platform and will be accustomed to the forms of behavior and rules of exactly that platform.

Hence, particularities of each platform should be transferred. However, if there are special solutions, special interaction concepts can be developed.

Throughout all employed systems interaction behaviors need to be the same. Therefore it has now become standard practice to refrain from designing a strict style guide and provide a pattern library, an icon library and design style guide instead. The design can only be roughly defined as there are diverse platforms and programming languages that do not offer the same design options.

Within the area of services, conduct and values, rules and processes are defined. For customer interfaces there are separate requirements for user interfaces (touch points).

In order to enable consistency in future projects, we will address various requirements.

2.4.1 Pattern Library

A pattern library specifies basic rules of interaction and behaviors for a product

- When a button is pressed, what happens?
- When an "edit" icon is pressed, what happens?
- The save button is always displayed on the right position.
- ...

Interaction behaviors additionally are comprised of graphics and clear rules in order to make it more understandable for the actual implementation.

Patterns or rules ensure a consistent interaction model across different platforms even when there are different designs or concepts behind it. Consistency within the product is crucial.

A typical structure of such a code of behavior would be as follows:

- Expressive title/headline,
- **Code of Behavior**,
- Description,
- Exceptions,
- Examples,
- Additional Information,
- Tips.

The codes of behavior must not be descriptive texts but should show clearly defined statements and procedures. A pattern has to be a book of reference and not a novel that is being read during working hours. Efficiency is very important in this context.

2.4.2 Icon Library

A icon library ensures that the same icons are used for a product, a product family or across all products of an organization in order to create one consistent external appearance, Fig. 2.16.

Especially when many teams are working on a specific product or on a product family, there are often various icons and diverse modes of representation chosen. Create an internal icon library for your product that is structured as follows:

- Title/name of the icon,
- **Icon (graphically depicted), download available in various sizes**,
- Description and meaning,
- Application examples,
- Additional information.

Fig. 2.16 CAMPUSonline Icons. Designed by youspi. (source: CAMPUSonline)

Example: Fig. 2.16.

Online icon libraries have a distinctive added value as all developers can quickly and easily access it. This means that the same icons can be used for the same functionality at all times. New icons are designed in the same icon style.

When it comes to the explanatory power of icons, it is recommended to try different designs for each target group.

A key is typically used as "Login" and "Logout" but it can for example, also be represented in other products such as "encrypt" and "decrypt". In such a case a customer-oriented icon design process that integrates the target group is strongly recommended.

2.4.3 Formula Style Guide

A formula style guide describes the basic interaction elements of a form and defines it with all its possibilities. When are check boxes, radio buttons, drop-downs and lists to be used?

Formula Style guides in Fig. 2.17 furthermore provide a clear direction for design purposes. What does a form with one column look like, as opposed to a form with two columns?

It's not the task of a form style guide that strictly defines and designs forms. This style guide creates consistency, but no process optimization or simplification of complex form designs. This is why a contextual analysis, workflow analysis and process optimization with the customer should be performed.

youspi
STYLE GUIDE
FORMULAR
CHECK BOX
FORM PANEL
GROUP BOX
RADIO BUTTON
BUTTONS
DROP-DOWN
INPUT FIELD
TEXT
DISABLED FIELD
ERROR HANDLING
TABS

Fig. 2.17 Form style guide

COLOR PALETTE
TYPOGRAPHY
ORANGE
ec6a24
VIOLET
382c3f
GREY
595f71
HEADER 1
Font: Liberation Sans Regular I Color: # ec6a24
HEADER 2
Font: Liberation Sans Regular I Color: # 382c3f
HEADER 3
Font: Liberation Sans Regular I Color: # 595f71

Fig. 2.18 Design Guideline

2.4.4 Design Style Guide

The design style guide in Fig. 2.18 specifies the main color features and design directions that are then employed across different platforms and programming techniques.

It is comprised of no more than three to four pages.

YOUR
DAILY
SOLUTION
GUIDE
youspi

Fig. 2.19 Your daily solution guide

2.4.5 Customer Experience Touch Book

For all processes and services with customer interaction there is the possibility to create a customer experience profile. In such a profile the interaction possibilities are defined for various touch points.

Strict rules of conduct are defined but many employees cannot identify with them as everybody has different strengths and communication skills.

The CX touch book in Fig. 2.19 defines certain requirements per touch point to ensure the company's philosophy is being applied. Nevertheless, the core of these touch books are the opportunities and freedoms that are given to the employees who in turn can create experiences for the customers. It needs to be noted that a solid customer or service analysis is indispensable as a first step to creating such a touch book.

- Example: Touch point Service:
- Situation,
- Typical Procedure,
- Frame for complaints,
- Other options.

Image: Your daily solution guide!

2.5 No Information Creates Simplicity

The best user interface is the one that has no user interface.
The best service is the one that is not visible at all.

In the gaming industry the functionalities and complexities are greater than for a business product. Nonetheless, there are thousands of people who play diverse games for several hours per day and enjoy themselves while doing so.

How is information presented in a game?

Regardless of which game we look at, only a certain game section will be shown on the screen. A game is divided into levels and tasks. Only the current critical information is being displayed and within 10 seconds, the surface can already look completely different.

The game player will easily cope with such a situation since the basic rules and interactions he is familiar with remain the same throughout the entire game. If new functionalities are added they fit into the context of the game and can be assigned immediately. Of course, these new interactions do not all appear at once but have to be earned or appear over time with every new level. Thus, an overload is avoided.

It is an intuitive game.

This way of thinking can also be applied to a wide variety of business products and processes.

Reduce to the essential:

The user does not need the entire amount of information at every point in time. Reduce to the essential. 80 % of the target group will be completely satisfied with 20 % of the functionalities or information.

This 80/20 rule was also applied by Youspi for the product development of the **Trendcorder**. It is an industrial product that controls, records and analyzes a variety of sensors of hardware. NASA is employing this product to measure vibrations and heat. Long-term measurements are made to ensure that no damage happens during the main operation of the equipment or systems.

The workflow is divided in a way that the sensors always have to be set at the beginning. The heart of the product however, is the recording and analysis of data. Hence the heart of the software is instantly visible after accessing it.

Record, stop, and pause are always immediately accessible.

As soon as an interaction is started, the navigation bar on the right side appears where the most important 20 % of all features are visible. If an expert wants to delve deeper, the menu can be pulled further to the left side, giving access to all the detail settings. It is a very simple concept that was awarded as the Product of the year 2014 by NASA, Fig. 2.20. Furthermore, the product was nominated for the Austrian Economic Oscar.

In advertising, it is imperative to bring the message to the point and to only convey the information that can be absorbed by the target audience.

Once a company has reached a point where is does not have to rely on text to convey information but rather purely use graphics and icons, the target group will already have created many links and memories within the brain that active information will no longer be necessary. If you see white headphones, you are likely to think of a multinational corporation selling consumer electronics. If you see Santa Claus, your brain will most likely have established links to a certain beverage company.

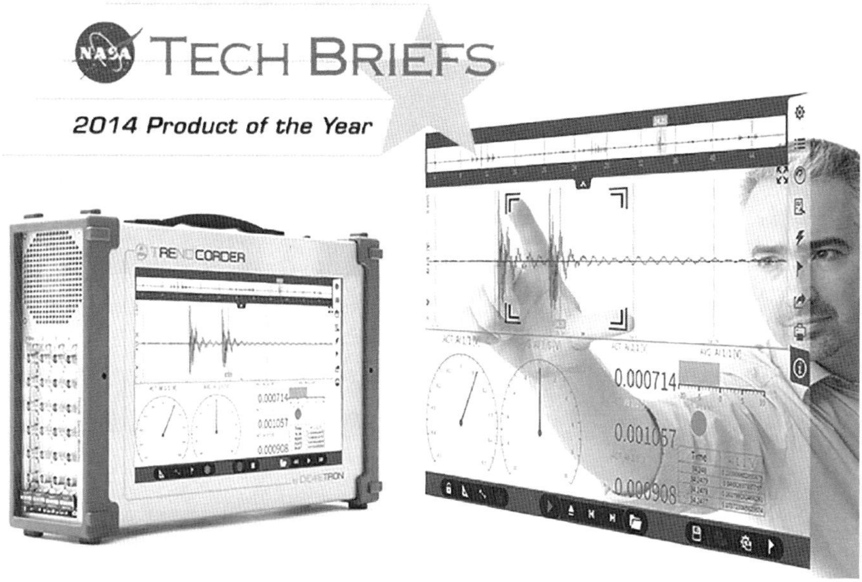
TECH BRIEFS
2014 Product of the Year
0.000714
0.001057
0.000908

Fig. 2.20 Trendcorder by DEWETRON, supported by youspi

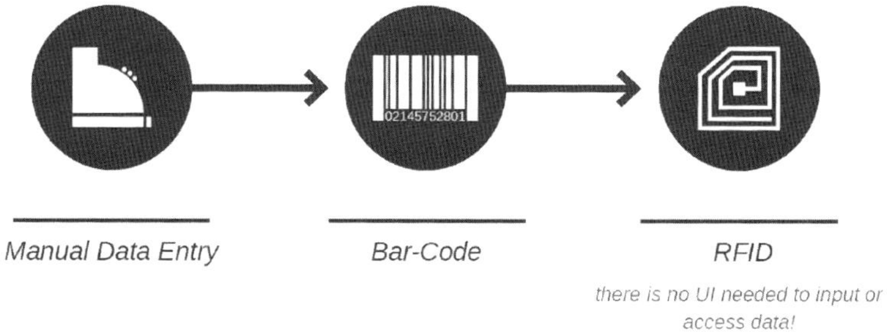
02145752801
Manual Data Entry
Bar-Code
RFID
there is no UI needed to input or access data!

Fig. 2.21 No interface is the best interface

Within the current era of the "Internet of Things", devices forward and process more information than ever before. This is a trend that will accelerate in the future meaning, the fewer the interfaces, the clearer and simpler things will become.

From the cash register to a barcode reader to a simple RFID chip, Fig. 2.21, – and already we are in and out of our local supermarket faster than ever. There are no more interfaces. All we have to do is press a payment confirmation button on our phones and the invoice will be billed to us.

Buy 34 €, Fig. 2.22.

Each touch point and every interaction with the customer gets rethought and redesigned in order for interfaces and interactions to be omitted and processes to be optimized. This also applies to business settings. In the overall context there will be

buy

Fig. 2.22 Buy Button

fewer interaction systems and we will increasingly specialize and restrict ourselves on certain systems. Nowadays, we are overwhelmed by too much information.

- How many times have you read an entire user manual?
- Who is familiar with all the functionalities of Excel and Word?
- How familiar are you with your car?

▶ Show the most important information only!

The next section comprises one of the most important lessons in this book.

2.6 Trust Through Information

Do you want to build trust? You have to build and earn it. Feedback and transparency are the main tools to create trust.

Let's start with a simple example: You are moving the mouse over a button. If the curser does not change, you can assume that the button does not work. As a consequence you send an e-mail to the service team complaining about it. You do not receive a confirmation that your mail was received or how long the processing may take. Thus, you assume that the company does not care about your complaint and you lose trust.

What is this about? The customer or user poses questions and is deflected from his actual goal creating user hurdles. This is how quickly a product or service is perceived as being complex or bad.

If a system has very long waiting times it is paramount to provide feedback to the user. Regardless of whether this is being expressed through a progress bar, an hourglass in a software solution or proper communication of current delays for arriving and departing flights on an airport, feedback is indispensable. When a customer does not receive feedback, a negative sentiment arises, especially if customer expectations are not met. However, if feedback and an open communication, ideally with a solution or substitute program, is provided early enough the negative situation can be transformed into a neutral or even a positive one.

Have you found yourself at a hotel reception asking a question and not receiving an answer even though the receptionist was standing directly in front of you? You probably repeated your question since your first enquiry apparently was not heard. Then, a disgruntled voice probably replied something along the lines of "I clearly heard you the first time. Can't you see I'm busy? Is it possible for you to wait for a minute?"

This is how easy a negative experience is created. By draining the positive holiday mood for a few minutes, or even hours it becomes very negative. If the receptionist had simply answered after the initial question, "I'll be with you in a minute or please wait a moment" everything would have been fine. Whenever possible it is highly recommendable to provide feedback that could potentially have positive impact.

► A feedback is a little effort on our side, put it potentially has a great impact on the overall experience.

Mindfulness and attention are not self-evident for many. One project team member may have had 'a bad day' and the consequence may be that not all use cases and scenarios are though through in the development phase, or that feedback is provided in such a way that only developers can understand. Misinterpretations may occur on several points in the communication.

► Attempt to thoroughly think through all possibilities of your system and aim at providing transparent feedback to the customer.
Try to be

- constructive,
- descriptive,
- concrete,
- positive.

If you provide the customer with an unexpected or incomplete feedback the user will be confused – such as if you click on a button and it suddenly disappears. What happened? An error?

2.6.1 Error Messages and Solutions

Error messages in different systems or forms are always a notable challenge. For each product you should differentiate in advance between:

- Indications,
- Uncritical error messages,
- Critical error messages.

Depending on the type of error message, these can be displayed differently in an interaction concept.

If errors appear the system should automatically offer solutions.

Put yourself back to your school days. You had to cope with dictations and math homework with the aim of developing your skills. You were dependent upon your teachers to a large extent because teachers are facilitators for students. If they tell their students what they are doing is not working without proposing a solution or an alternative approach students will easily get frustrated and may not learn. They will resort to asking friends or find another way of figuring it out on their own.

The exact thing happens with applications in which errors occur and solutions have to be found. How often have you received an error message that required your reading confirmation through pressing "OK" or "Cancel" and how often were you presented with a proposed solution to the problem at hand?

Feedback is a design opportunity to prevent customers or users from having negative thoughts. As long as the user has the feeling of being guided and being in control of everything there will be no negativity.

Let's look at another example: You want to buy a new pair of shoes and order a pair online. The order was sent and you are now waiting for your shoes without any feedback on when they will be delivered. Based on the information on the website and your past experience you believe that the shoes will arrive within five days after you ordered them. Thus, you can easily cope with five days. After eight days however, when the shoes still have not arrived how do you feel? What happened? Your expectations are not met and you now have a negative attitude towards the web shop. The shoes arrived after nine days.

How could this have been improved?

Again, you order a pair of shoes and are informed in the ordering process that it might take up to nine days until the shoes can be delivered due to of delivery problems. You now purchase the shoes and adjust your expectations. If you receive a notification on the ninth day that the shoes will be delivered one day later you may be a bit unhappy however, you were informed.

2.6.2 Feedback as Sense of Achievement and Confidence Increase

Through providing feedback you can generate a sense of achievement and confidence within your customers. As in project management you can redesign lengthy processes into living processes and thereby minimize the risk of process dropouts.

Split processes with more than seven steps into subtasks and always provide feedback at every step. This will allow you to achieve a quick sense of achievement from a psychological point of view.

An example that illustrates this well is the process steps in wizards or online surveys which are visible at all times. You are always aware of the steps you have already completed and how many steps still lie ahead of you.

Another example would be that we always expect to receive an order confirmation whenever we purchase something online. People require feedback as a confirmation that they have done something right.

> In the absence of feedback, uncertainty is created.
> As a consequence of uncertainty, everything comes to a standstill.

Standstills should be avoided by all means possible regardless of whether it comes to a product, a service, or a process. Through proper feedback you can motivate people and encourage them to run faster, jump higher and achieve more than they would have ever thought possible.

Every game works on this principle.

2.6.3 Gamification

In its essence gamification is positive feedback or feedback on the current status which you can compare with others. Regardless of whether the outcome is positive or negative, you know where you stand. Transparency is always given.

When we compare this to flirting we understand that flirting is only a human game that is all about feedback. When do I receive feedback and at which point do I receive negative feedback? People tend to practice this game a lot as long as they do not receive a negative feedback. We assume that the other person responds well to us and therefore move on. No feedback can be misunderstood.

Furthermore, every relationship thrives on feedback. If no honest feedback is provided negative aspects will be suppressed and potentially end in a disaster.

Gamification is mainly used in games but is slowly becoming popular within service and business contexts. However, there is vast potential for future developments of gamification approaches.

Example

In an organization there are about 100 technical products. The sales staff has to sell all products and the respective product managers supply them with highly technical information. The sales platform was now transformed into a pure communication tool for the sales team. Three areas were specified (Fig. 2.23):

1. For every product there are five questions and corresponding answers that are of prime interest for the sales team. Only sales staff are allowed to answer these questions, as they can answer them in their own language and to their best knowledge. For every answer they can earn points.
2. On a second level, all answers get rated by the sales staff themselves, again points can be earned.
3. The third area is a pure view that appears upon the login. Here the five highest rates responses are noted for every question and this is exactly the information the sales staff needs to properly sell the products.

Hence, the "secret information" of the sales staff was suddenly being shared, turning the project into a success story that was not only providing notable added value to the organization but moreover, facilitated the everyday work of the sales team tremendously.

To develop such concepts, you first have to understand the theory of motivation, conduct a needs-analysis and design a unique solution based on your findings. A solution cannot be simply applied to any given product, or organization. Internal processes and the work environment play a central role and more attention needs to be awarded to this fact. Indeed, one factor that often does not get sufficient attention is interpersonal relationships and people.

Let's move on to the two remaining rules of simplification of information.

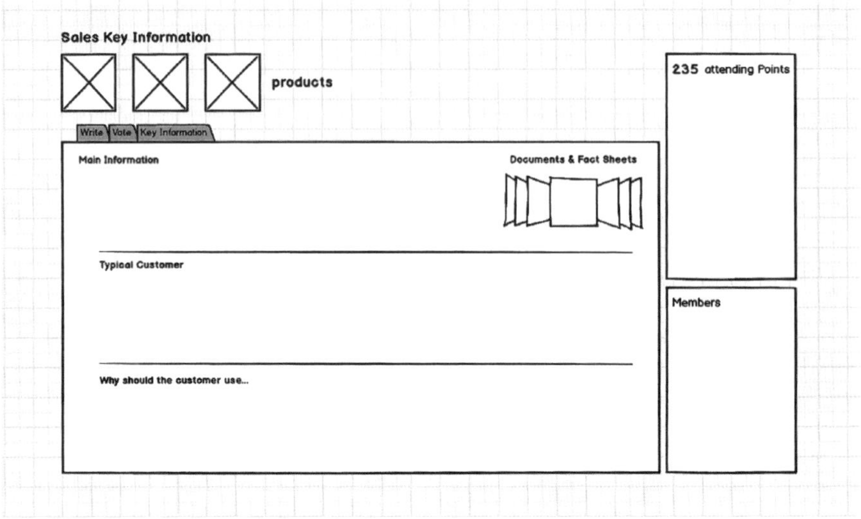
Sales Key Information
products
235 attending Points
Write
Vote
Key Information
Main Information
Documents & Fact Sheets
Typical Customer
Members
Why should the customer use...

Fig. 2.23 Sales Application of a major organization. Supported by youspi

2.7 Design Influences the Emotional Value

Design takes on an important part in affecting the human perception and the first impression. However, design can only partially improve the usability of a product.

Design can provide guidelines. With a solid color scheme or a proper usage of design elements, the user can be guided along processes and services. Therefore design supports the concept phase and allows highlighting or neglecting specific elements.

Design can turn a product into a WOW-product instead of keeping it simply as an efficient and neutrally simple product. Hence, design does not increase usability but rather has a range of other effects:

- Design increases the emotional value of a product.
- Design increases the actual value of a product.
- Design makes products consistent.
- Design appeals to the target audience.
- Design can be a purchase decision.
- Design can be emotionally binding.
- Design can be added value in comparison to the competition.

Concept and design need to be clearly distinguished at this point.

Let's look at a product that is not user-friendly. A new design will probably make it more appealing to the eye, but it will not make it more intuitive.

Now, if a user-friendly product with an excellent interaction concept gets a new look and feel it will remain user-friendly.

An icon may be beautifully designed however, if it does not dispose of the visual language and convey the information a user can process, the best design could be for nothing.

What do the icons in Fig. 2.24 tell you?

A visual language can be learned and apparent to a majority of users or it can be very specific to the target group. The design itself provides little support for the actual message. True significance is achieved through the concept.

Example

In 2010 Youspi developed a first-use user manual for a Philips epilator. The challenge in this project was to work solely with images, as the product had to be sold internationally and translation costs needed to be saved.

A concept of images was created, which was first evaluated in a usability test with different people from the target group. In the second testing phase, an AB testing was carried out which is a comparative test between two variations: the new instruction as opposed to the image-text manual that was used before the re-design, Fig. 2.25.

Fig. 2.24 Icons

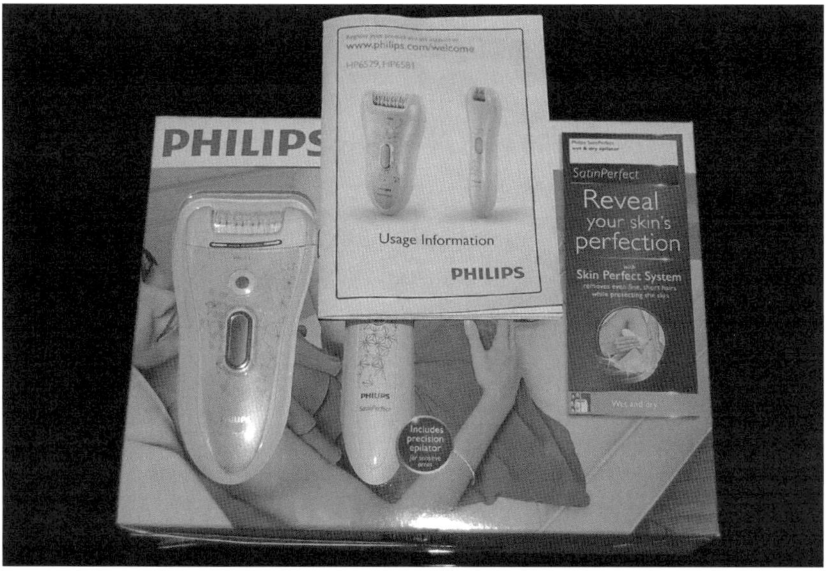
www.philips.com/welcome
Usage Information
PHILIPS
SatinPerfect
Reveal
your skin's
perfection
Skin Perfect System
Includes
precision
epilator

Fig. 2.25 Philips First-Use User Manual, supported by youspi. (source: Philips)

1
2
3

Fig. 2.26 Headline (source: Philips)

As a consequence an image manual was created which could have been produced in a variety of designs since the imagery was evaluated in usability tests and was considered to be very good and clear.

How are headings presented in such a solution? See Fig. 2.26.

Do you know what to do?

Simple manuals can become your 'reason to believe'. Have you ever thought about this?

Let's look at a different example. Landing pages for mobile applications. The website's only objective should be to convince the customer to click on a link, purchase the application, or download it. Consequently the landing page's heart is a button. BUT: A button will seldom be a proper motivation to buy. Therefore, an emotional incentive must be found through which the design can be created. Design has effect.

Have a look at a little trick within the provision of information. Aimed at coloring action buttons which are linked to the main use case, are always in a contrarian color to the rest of the system. You will quickly realize that the customer will follow your suggested path more easily, Fig. 2.27.

Attempt to use design as a persuasion tool, instead of as a mere creative element.

2.8 Simplify for the Human Perception

You walk into an electronics store and want to buy a camera. You want to make the right decision and ask a salesman for some detailed advice. After half an hour you know exactly what type of camera you need and you have narrowed your selection to two possible cameras. The prices are similar however one camera appears to be more complex in its functionality.

Which one will you choose?

Although at first advice may be desired, first impressions count. Simplicity happens through the mind and not through descriptions.

► "Simple" means something different to everybody

On the web, your websites have exactly 50 milliseconds to create a first impression (Lindgaard et al. 2006).

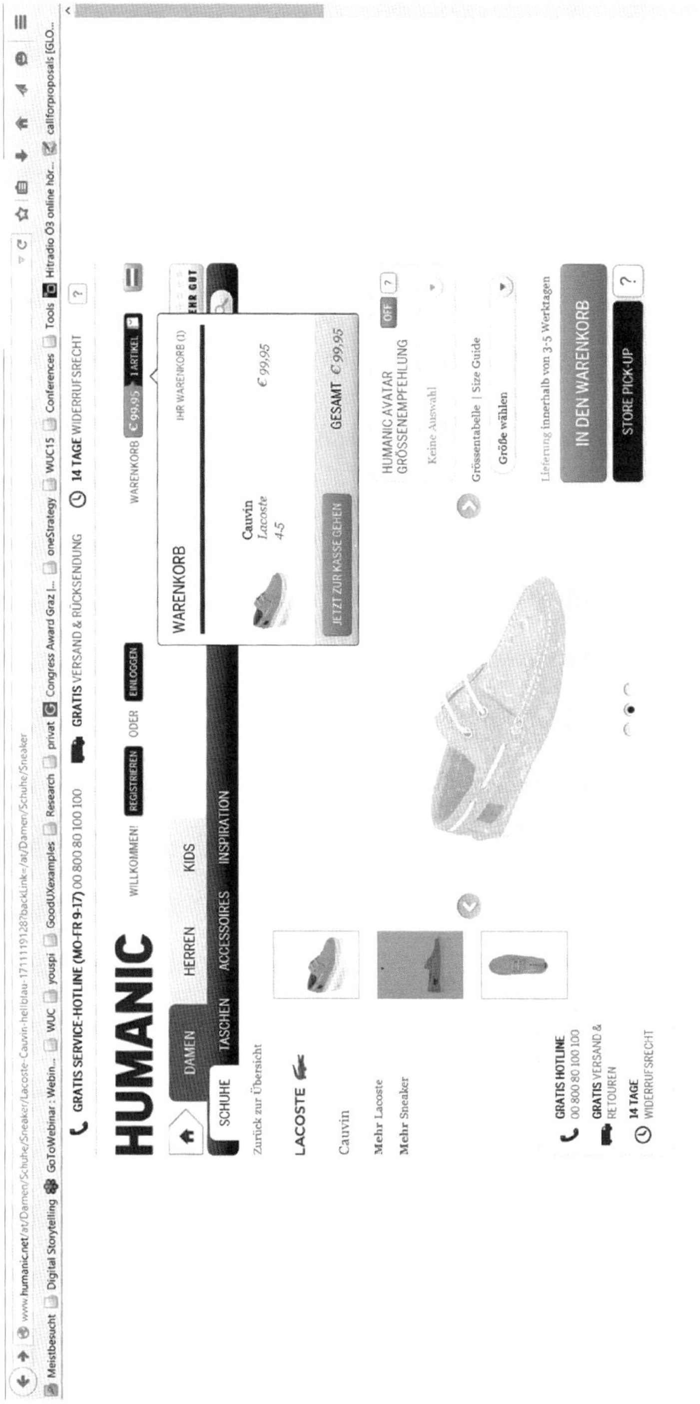
www.humanic.net/at/Damen/Schuhe/Sneaker/Lacoste-Cauvin-hellblau-171111191287backLink=/at/Damen/Schuhe/Sneaker
GRATIS SERVICE-HOTLINE (MO-FR 9-17) 00 800 80 100 100
GRATIS VERSAND & RÜCKSENDUNG
14 TAGE WIDERRUFSRECHT
HUMANIC
WILLKOMMEN!
REGISTRIEREN
ODER
EINLOGGEN
WARENKORB
€ 99,95
1 ARTIKEL
DAMEN
HERREN
KIDS
SCHUHE
TASCHEN
ACCESSOIRES
INSPIRATION
WARENKORB
IHR WARENKORB (1)
Cauvin
Lacoste
45
€ 99,95
JETZT ZUR KASSE GEHEN
GESAMT € 99,95
Zurück zur Übersicht
LACOSTE
Cauvin
Mehr Lacoste
Mehr Sneaker
HUMANIC AVATAR
GRÖSSENEMPFEHLUNG
OFF
Keine Auswahl
Grössentabelle | Size Guide
Größe wählen
Lieferung innerhalb von 3-5 Werktagen
IN DEN WARENKORB
STORE PICK-UP
GRATIS HOTLINE
00 800 80 100 100
GRATIS VERSAND & RETOUREN
14 TAGE
WIDERRUFSRECHT

Fig. 2.27 Screenshot of Humanic website (source: Humanic)

SCUBA
SCUBA

Fig. 2.28 Example of showing a product (source: scubadiving 2015)

If the first impression is upgradeable you have almost no chance of keeping visitors on your site or of convincing them to return unless you have an outstanding content.

In order to create a great first impression, you will need two things:

- Relevant content,
- A stunning design (emotionally appealing).

In this regard, you have to pay attention to the fact that at every customer interface, the HALO effect comes into play (Wells 1907). This means that the first impression is always generalized. If a customer interface is great it is assumed that all other aspects of the company are excellent as well. Nonetheless, if a user gets caught within the only customer interface that you did not pay attention to, he is likely to doubt your entire organization. Is this what you want?

► To simplify your products and services for human perception do not present all features and facts from the start. At first, show the most necessary elements and aim at delivering additional information in small portions. This way, you can easily create a multitude of small achievements. Provide more information, when more information is requested.

Applying this to a software product means that the most important information needs to be clearly visible right upon the first access of the software. Create your own demos to show the functionalities and put an emphasis on making product photos clear, comprehensible and emotional, Fig. 2.28.

This iPad is presented to be sold. What does your iPad look like? Mine has have a lot more applications does not look as basic. Five to eight pages filled with applications, folders and subpages. However, when selling such an iPad, it is crucial to use product images that make it look simple and easily comprehensible.

In fact, it is recommended to show the customer the optimal case and the most beautiful perspective of products. The first impression needs to be good and simple. However, the customer should never be over promised as this will lead to frustration at a later stage.

Human perception can quickly be deceived. Candid reduction in sales is now commonplace.

Let's compare the presented simplification rules and approaches to the fundamentals of the design of dialogues according to ISO.

2.9 Design of Dialogues vs Your Own Rules

Now compare the design of dialogues with the approach that was just illustrated. Both methods achieve the same goal: to simplify and better design products and processes.

It's up to you to determine which approach works best and will be chosen in the future, Table 2.1.

We see that both approaches lead to the same joint goal. The path put forward in this book is to cover several principles of the ISO standard. In the future we recommend you to use those tools you feel most comfortable with and where you see the greatest benefit for your work.

The last two chapters of simplicity focus primarily on design. We learn that among other things, design can emotionalize through colors and shapes. Still, there are other tools to spark emotions, as well. These will be discussed in greater detail in the following section.

Table 2.1 Compare dialog principles with our approach

	Heart beat	Persona	Consis-tence	Priori-tization	No Info	Feed-back	Design	Percep-tion
Suitability for the task	×			×	×			×
Self-descrip-tiveness			×				×	
Suitability for Learning	×	×	×	×		×	×	
Controllability				×		×	×	
Conformity with user ex-pectations	×	×	×		×		×	×
Customizability			×				×	
Error Tolerance	×	×	×			×		

References

http://www.amazon.de/, accessed on April 2015

Google 2008, http://www.google.at, accessed on October 2013

Google 2013, https://www.google.at accessed on January 2013

Google 2015, http://www.google.at. accessed on January 2015

http://www.scubadiving.com/new-ipad-wallpapers-scuba-diving, accessed on April 2015

Lindgaard, G., Fernandes, G., Dudek, C., and Brown, J. (2006). Attention web designers: Behaviour and Information Technology, You have 50 milliseconds to make a good first impression! 25(2), 115–126.

Rawlinson, G. E.: The significance of letter position in word recognition, Unpublished PhD Thesis, Psychology Department, University of Nottingham, Nottingham (1976)

Wells, F. L. (1907). A Statistical Study of Literary Merit. *Archives of Psychology*, 1–30.

Towards Emotions and Experience 3

Now we are familiar with the art of simplification and the profession of usability with all the activities involved. Assuming the expectations of the end customers are not very high, even simple products and services can become an experience. But, if simplicity is a prerequisite for a product or service, how can we now go on, as required by the use of the terms 'User **Experience**' and 'Customer **Experience**', to create experiences? In this chapter you will explore ways and means of quickly and easily creating experiences in order to bring customers under your spell, thereby creating a sales experience.

There are three ways to influence people emotionally with products and services. We start with the simplest possibility:

1. **Emotional appeal.**

The next stage is for a person to experience

2. **Emotional excitement.**

But these are just static, short-term options. Long-term influence is based on a person experiencing

3. **Emotional bonding.**

To use these three methods to influence human behavior, we must first understand emotions and what causes them. As a first step, let us go back to cognitive psychology.

► **The Rule is** The more sensory channels that are addressed, the better the learning.

The more diverse the ways in which we learn, the more diverse the ways in which we remember and store the information. Consequently, the recall rate increases significantly if more senses are involved in the learning process (Fig. 3.1):

- Hearing only: 20 %,
- Seeing only: 30 %,

J. Robier, *UX Redefined*, Management for Professionals, DOI 10.1007/978-3-319-21062-9_3

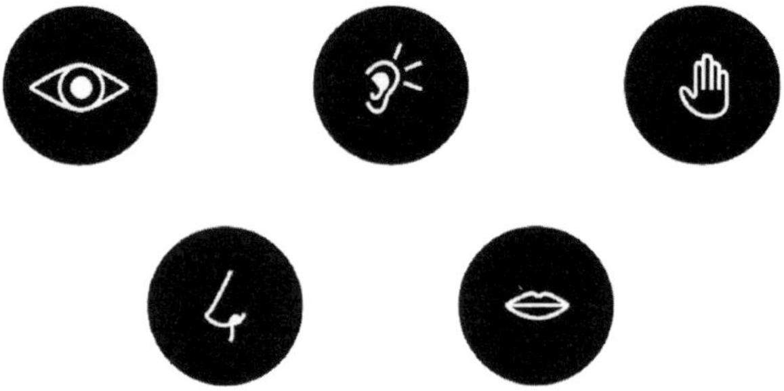

Fig. 3.1 Senses

- Seeing and hearing: 50 %,
- Seeing, hearing and discussing: 70 %,
- Seeing, hearing, discussing and rehearsing: 90 % (Friedl 2013).

I can agree with these findings under one condition only:

I am interested!

If I am not interested in what I do, these figures mean nothing. I need to take just one example from my college days: Exams were coming up, it was warm and sunny, the beach volleyball court was not too far way, and I had to study accounting.

What was the context?

I was interested in everything but my study subject. I wanted to motivate myself to at least read and study 20 pages. First page, second page, third page … What happened? I could not remember the sentence that I had just read, even though I was motivated. I had read it out loud, seen and heard it, but still remembered nothing. I was simply not interested.

Interest and motivation can move mountains.

Can you imagine an 80-year-old person learning Chinese? It would probably be very difficult. But if this person suddenly meets the love of their life from China, it probably will not take long until they speak their first Chinese words.

> We learn only what is necessary to us.
> If you want to develop your potential, you must
> keep up your enthusiasm.
> Gerald Hüther

The human brain weighs about 1.4 kilograms – that's only 2 percent of our bodyweight – but it uses more than 20 percent of our body's energy (Roth 2001).

This shows us how strong and powerful our brains can be. A toddler experiences a state of excitement between 20 and 50 times per day. Each of these small rushes and experiences triggers a torrent of processes in their brains that are especially needed for growth and restructuring of neuronal networks (Hüther 2011)

This is why it is also very important for children to stay busy. All these experiences are stored in our frontal lobe, which makes up one third of the brain, Fig. 3.2.

The frontal lobe is the center of our emotional network ("How did I experience it?") and our cognitive network ("That's how I experienced it.").

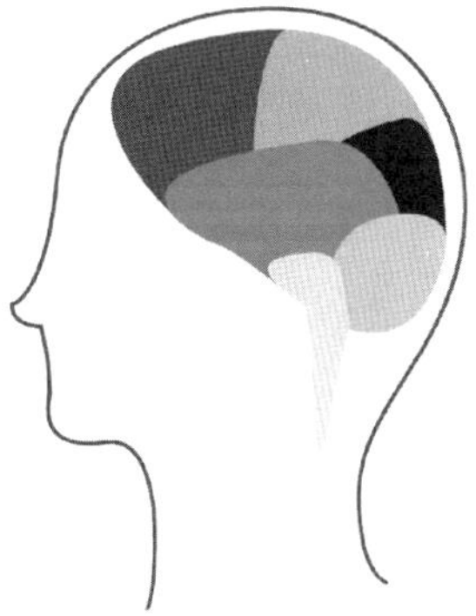

Fig. 3.2 Areas of the brain

So this includes our (Antosik 2011):

1. Emotions and
2. Experiences.

If I want to influence people's behavior, I must combine emotions and experiences. They both affect us and can change acquired structures.

Our needs give rise to our motivation to act. What we experience can excite us, which in turn creates an emotional link. So we can draw the conclusion that

... **relationships** are crucial, **not contents**

... **experiences** are crucial, **not contents**

But what is an **experience?**

Experiences always revolve around people. Only people can perceive and share experiences.

Experiences are always emotional!

For example, take a sunrise. A sunrise is a recurring event that displays new color variations every morning, depending on various environmental factors. Viewed soberly, a sunrise is no emotional experience. Only the connection with other events, for example, standing on a cliff in warm southern breeze with your partner, can make it an experience. There is good reason why people describe such events with breathtaking vividness. This creates an experience.

► Only when we connect emotions with an event does it become an experience.

These experiences, these magic "wow moments", take place in our heads. We cannot **create experiences**. We can only support and create the **conditions** for generating such experiences. We can design **interfaces and interactions** to trigger customer experiences. If you can give 80 % of your customers an experience every time, you are creating experiences. It's possible. But more on that later.

How can I influence people without knowing their needs?

3.1 Emotional Appeal

The simplest method is to work **with instinctive psychological** influence strategies, which include:

- People,
- Children and animals,
- Food and eating,
- Fear,
- Repetition and sympathy,
- Humor in advertising,
- Sexuality in advertising,
- Credibility of people.

These are also themes often used in advertising. They allow you to easily access all human emotions, since they move us and appeal to our emotions.

Mascots are large stuffed animals that always appeal to us and that we consider "kind", Fig. 3.3.

With these basic emotions, emotional messages can be quickly transmitted. People process 95 percent of environmental information subconsciously (Zaltman 2003).

Fig. 3.3 Mascot of the Styrian athletics organisation STLV

Hirter
Hirter Fasstypen
www.hirterbier.at

Fig. 3.4 Ad for the the beer brand Hirter (source: marketing-gui 2015)

WHY IS IT SO HARD
TO SEE BLACK AND BLUE

Fig. 3.5 Ad that uses the emotion of fear

- Colors are **subconsciously** emotional.
  They create emotional patterns.
  Use these subconscious dimensions to excite people, Fig. 3.6.

How can I trigger emotions using facts?

100

The number 100 is just a fact that causes no emotions, because we connect nothing to it. The number 13 is a different case; many see it as lucky (or unlucky).

100

Died in an accident.

But if we read words after the number 100, we become emotionalized.

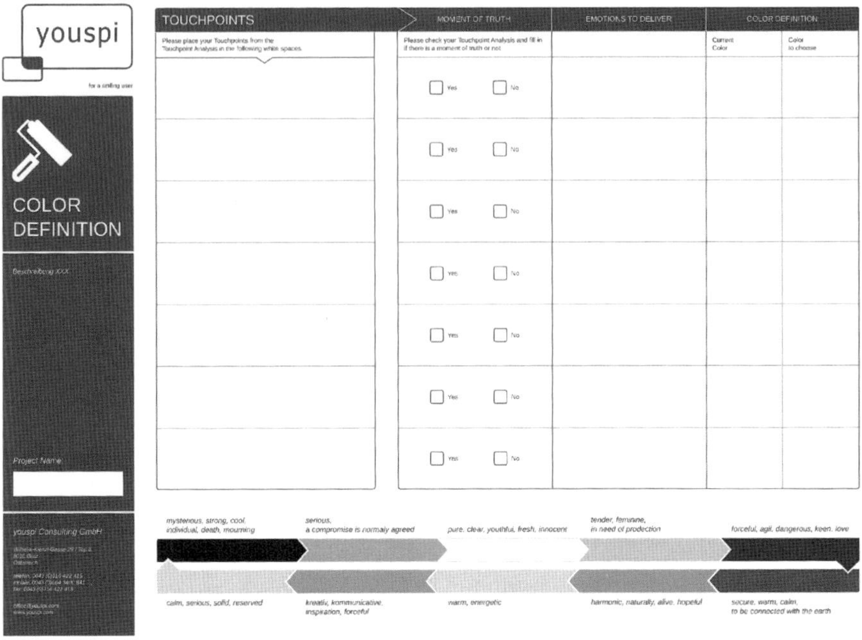
youspi
COLOR DEFINITION
Project Name:
TOUCHPOINTS
Please place your Touchpoints from the Touchpoint Analysis in the following white spaces
MOMENT OF TRUTH
Please check your Touchpoint Analysis and fill in if there is a moment of truth or not
Yes
No
EMOTIONS TO DELIVER
COLOR DEFINITION
Current Color
Color to choose
mysterious, strong, cool, individual, death, mourning
serious, a compromise is normaly agreed
pure, clear, youthful, fresh, innocent
tender, feminine, in need of prodection
forceful, agil, dangerous, keen, love
calm, serious, solid, reserved
kreativ, kommunicative, inspiration, forceful
warm, energetic
harmonic, naturally, alive, hopeful
secure, warm, calm, to be connected with the earth

Fig. 3.6 Touchpoint Color Definition

100

Died in an accident.
Many children lost their parents.
One of them was named Tim.

If TIM, twelve years, was followed by the words YOUR SON, could you imagine the rest?

You can try using stories and anecdotes to emotionalize facts and target people emotionally.

If you think about instinctive strategies or walk through life with open eyes tomorrow, you will see hundreds of different influences affecting you.

The next stage is emotional excitement.

3.2 Emotional Excitement

The next higher ability, but also difficulty, is to excite people emotionally. Therefore, let's look at the dimensions of excitement:

- Surprise,
- Perceived appreciation,

- Distinction,
- Experience.

These dimensions cannot be targeted emotionally with individual images; here we need personal contact or long-term processes/services. These types of excitement can occur or be used in any private or job-related situation.

3.2.1 Surprise

- Something unexpected, which far exceeds my expectations (service, function ...).
- A surprise at having underestimated something.
- A photo showing a situation to which I feel intimate emotional attachment and which provides a whole new perspective.

Example

You are a business traveler always staying at the same hotels, because your company books them. Unfortunately, your doctor recently diagnosed you with lactose intolerance. Now you are again traveling but feel that this could be somewhat of a challenge for your hotels. Having arrived in Switzerland, you present your case at the reception. After reminding them politely at breakfast, you get what you need without any further problems.

Three weeks later, you travel to Las Vegas. You expect that you will have to remind the staff. However, the receptionist addresses you right away about your issue at the previous hotel and tells you it should be no problem. You are surprised that your information has traveled around the world and that you have received such personal support. This enormously increases your loyalty towards the hotel chain.

Surprises are always connected to expectations. They can be predictable – or not. They can also directly prepare people and give hints arousing their curiosity. Every good movie has a plot that makes viewers expect one outcome but then delivers another. A surprising ending usually makes a good movie.

Personal appreciation is another deep-seated feeling that allows us to excite people.

3.2.2 Perceived Appreciation (Personalization)

- You feel understood and respected.
- Feel sincere personal interest.
- Being seen as an individual, not as part of a faceless mass.

Involving customers in product and service development through joint meetings for new ideas and innovations (co-creation) can trigger excitement.

Officially inviting customers to work with you increases their perceived appreciation. Seeing them off with a "thank you" lets you excite them additionally. This can strongly enhance customer loyalty to your company.

Excitement is possible in any project. Involve those people that are relevant. Draw a stakeholder map to find out who these people are.

Perceived appreciation can be found in many CRM systems. My bank sends me an automated text message for my birthday. "How lovely!" (Ironically). Of course, I would prefer that they didn't message me at all. I feel none of the perceived appreciation that this is supposed to show.

People you barely know remembering your name makes you happy. It lets you feel that your name is worth something.

Try to approach a person you casually know with respect and care. You will notice that personal appreciation has a high value in our society, which is forgotten by many.

So we meet many people who might seem to act strangely. That can be positive, but also negative.

3.2.3 Distinction

- Being different from the rest.
- Enjoying things, having access to them.
- Sticking out from the crowd.

Being different from the rest in the business world takes a lot of courage or a clear goal and a vision. You must be a pioneer, an innovator. The line between "genius and insanity" or between "loved and hated" is very thin.

Customer interfaces offer many opportunities here. As soon as expectations are exceeded, we can speak of distinction. After thoroughly analyzing customer needs, creative methods like the Lotus Blossom technique by Yasuo Matsumura – Fig. 3.7 – are always helpful:

1. Write the central challenge into the center of a circle.
2. Write the significant solutions, components or dimensions of the challenge into the eight areas towards the edges of the circle.
3. Start again and try to find new areas for the eight initial ones.

This lets you find structured solutions and ideas, which you can then prioritize in various ways.

For years, "Franz" was a unique phenomenon in Austrian shoe retail advertising, Fig. 3.8. Everyone knew these exceptional advertisements!

Distinction should be used in all areas of management and at all customer touchpoints. Are your customers unhappy or do you need to solve minor issues with

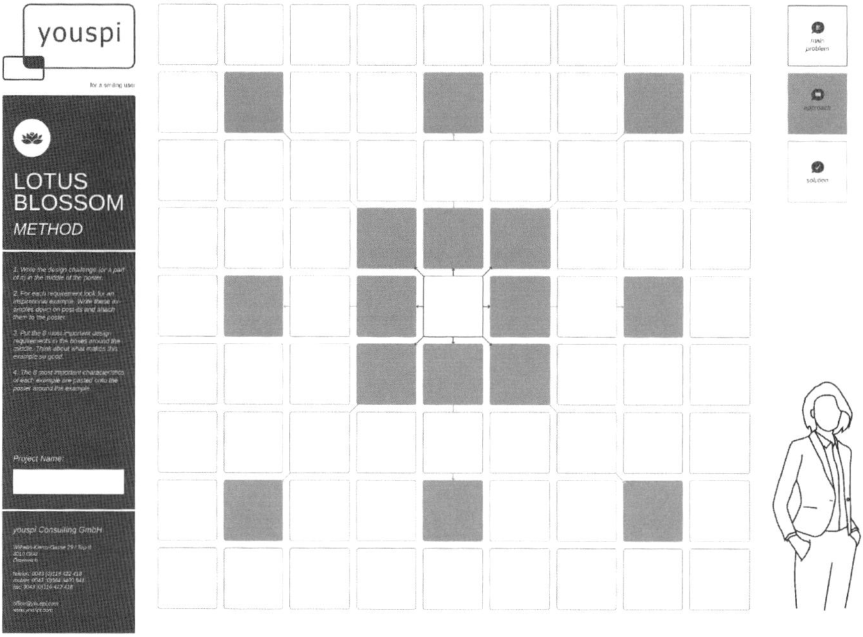
youspi
LOTUS
BLOSSOM
METHOD
Project Name:

Fig. 3.7 Lotus Blossom method

them? Distinction, paired with personality and a little humor, can often work miracles.

Example

A bus company had repeated difficulties getting people to move to the back when the buses were full. When many people entered at the front, they stayed there, creating a jam. So the standing spaces in the buses are always crammed in one section only. The bus driver always had to ask people to move to the rear; people who entered crammed in and became dissatisfied. The people in the bus did not want to be pushed to the back; so we have three unsatisfied target groups. How can you influence this emotionally – whether positively or negatively – to solve the problem?

Do you have an idea?

The bus company had long creative sessions and conducted a customer analysis for its target group to find the right solution, Fig. 3.9.

In another project, a company tried collecting e-mail addresses for a sweepstakes during an event. There was wonderful advertising for a mobile campaign, where participants got a 2D code directing them to a website, where they had to answer one question and then enter their data.

The problem was that the process customers had to go through was much too complicated.

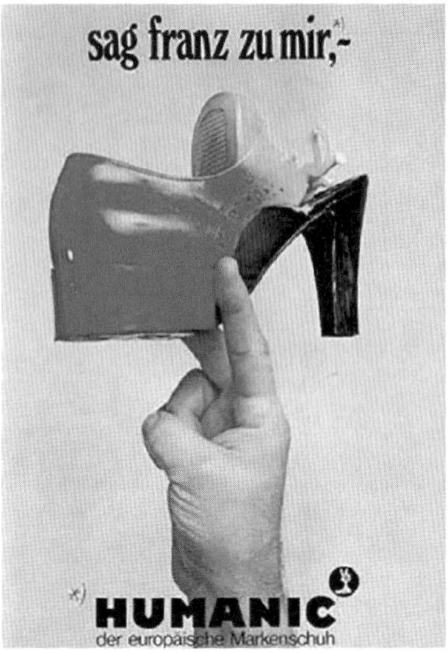
sag franz zu mir,-
HUMANIC
der europäische Markenschuh

Fig. 3.8 Call me Franz (source: Humanic)

- They had no 2D code readers on their phones.
- The link sometimes did not work.
- They received no confirmation e-mail.
- etc. ...

During a different event, we had a similar task: to collect e-mail addresses. For this, we designed a digital image wall. It was similar to those at the circus, where you stick your head through a hole in a cardboard picture and get your photo taken. We used the same principle on a 43″ multi-touch screen: You stand in front of the

ATTENTION
All people with
CLEAN
underwear, please
move to the rear

Fig. 3.9 Attention, all people with CLEAN underwear, please move to the rear

www.ottakringer.at
Anton und Otto meinen:
„So sehen echte Ottakringer aus!“
Warum erfrischt mich das Ottakringer bloss so? Bloss so

Fig. 3.10 Ottakringer campaign

screen, a camera inserts your head into the company's theme and then you press the trigger switch. After five seconds, the camera takes your photo. Then you enter your e-mail address into the touch screen to receive your photo, Fig. 3.10.

What's the advantage of such an application?

For the customer:

- Personal interaction (getting involved),
- Personal appeal through the photograph.

This makes it easier to give out your e-mail address

For the company:

- Integration of their own brand.
- Associating the brand with something funny.

This campaign had an ROI of 30 % above average, requiring just 1/10 of the usual budget.

Example

A small provincial town; the local car workshop has the problem that customers always want to be there during the first inspection and even watch the mechanics make small repairs. Of course, customers always have loads of questions:

- "Why are you doing this?"
- "Why are you doing it differently than I am used to?"
- "Why are you doing it at all?"

Price list:
45 $/h - Car repair
60 $/h - Repairs & watching
75 $/h - Repairs & giving advice

Fig. 3.11 Repairs sign

Every customer believes themselves to be an expert. That's not so bad, at a basic level, but it takes the mechanics an added ten minutes per hour; added up over a day, over a month, this significantly affects their performance. With the help of an acquaintance, the workshop developed solutions for "annoying" customers. In Fig. 3.11 is what they came up with.

This fixed the problem very quickly; the mechanics were now able to fully concentrate on their work.

However, large companies can also personalize their product development by creating and building modifications. The following example (Nike, Fig. 3.12) shows a distinction strategy in the shoe business, which also works for cars, motorcycles or wedding rings. Personalization, i. e. increasing personal value, relies heavily on customer experience.

Studies show that 86 % of customers would pay more for products and services, if companies offered them an experience (Markmann 2013).

So, we come to our fourth point: experiences and memories. How to increase customer experience by linking it to prior knowledge or memories.

3.2.4 Experiences/Memories

- Evoke previous experiences.
- Use meaningful metaphors.
- Use previous situations as emotional triggers.
- Tell stories.

When evoking experiences, you use people's individual knowledge. If you have a campaign that's been successful for several years, you can start from there. If you had a type of chocolate that tastes great, you wouldn't change this successful product. Just using the same wrapper color in other products could trigger associations with the delicious chocolate.

Historical elements or celebrities are often used in advertising. A successful person with a certain degree of celebrity attracts more attention than an unknown one. I would like to name just one very successful example.

Shoot it,
Choose it,
Own it.
Inspiration is everywhere.
NIKEiD. App now available for iPhone

Fig. 3.12 Nike Ad

Example

Gatorade Replay – Fig. 3.13 – tells the story of a final game between two high school football teams that ended in a tie. The two high schools cultivate a traditional football rivalry. Gatorade organized a repetition of the game with the same players at the same location fifteen years later.

Gatorade is relying on the memory of a game that was tied after a year-long rivalry. This game was bound to evoke emotions. Gatorade also employs distinction, as never before has there been such a replay. All locals were emotionally included.https://www.youtube.com/watch?v=xQWSsfluZI8https://www.youtube.com/watch?v=xQWSsfluZI8: Fig. 3.14.

What was the outcome of this game?

More than 20,000 tickets were sold within a very short time.

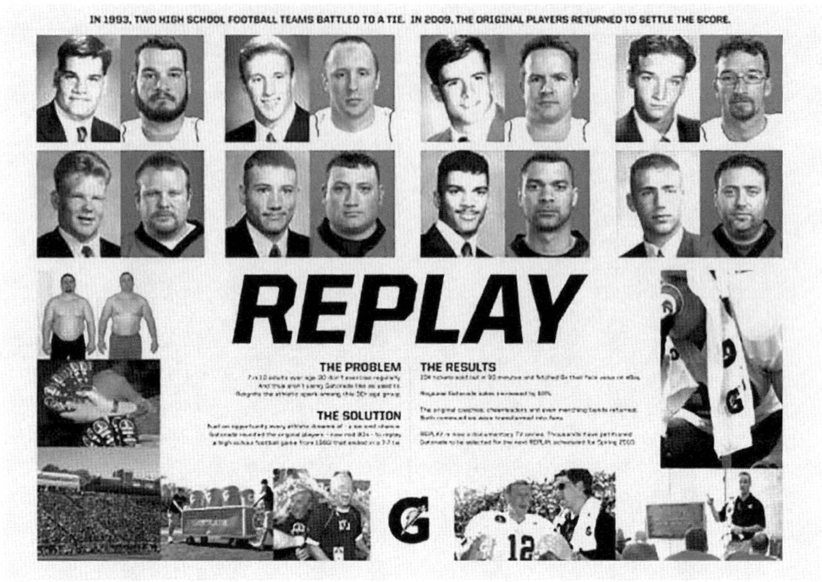
IN 1993, TWO HIGH SCHOOL FOOTBALL TEAMS BATTLED TO A TIE. IN 2009, THE ORIGINAL PLAYERS RETURNED TO SETTLE THE SCORE.
REPLAY
THE PROBLEM
THE SOLUTION
THE RESULTS

Fig. 3.13 Gatorade Adverts (PepsiCo 2010)

Fig. 3.14 2D Code for the YouTube link above

- \$ 3,415,255 of media exposure generated, spending just \$ 255,000.
- Replay became one of CNN's Top Stories in 2009.
- Replay became a TV series reaching 90 million households.
- Regional Gatorade sales rose by 63 %.

Do **not** search for the right message or the medium for transmitting your contents. You need no new technology or old methods! Do not hold on to dogmas like "print advertising is all I need." Customers pay for **stories and needs**, not for functions or cool communication channels. You achieve success by connecting with people emotionally.

3.3 Emotional Bonding

We ask how to best prepare information so that our brain can process it. Storytelling is a technique used for thousands of years in all cultures, so our brains are adapted to it.

> We do not have 30 secs to be interrupted by advertising but, however, when audiences are exposed to content that is valuable, entertaining, emotive and simply enjoyable – even if it's branded – they miraculously have 30 minutes to watch and then share the content with their own audiences (Mark Scaefer).

► Storytelling is the best alternative to first-hand experience.

Storytelling is a method of consuming and remembering information ideally adapted to humans.

> One of evolution's genial strokes is to process, store and share information in the form of stories. Only this way can our brain, with its 100 billion nerve cells, create patterns that let us make predictions, thus helping us procreate, adapt and survive (Fuchs 2006).

Many types of information preparation can facilitate storytelling:

- Good design tells stories,
- Good content and
- Good strategies tell stories.

To share information about products or services, we normally use facts. Who remembers facts? Who tells other people stories about a product or a service?

> Products and services always have an end. The deeper value lies in their story (Arne van Oosterom).

Facts alone tell us nothing. All information has an end, i. e., it does not enter our long-term memory quickly or easily. There are too few associations for our brain to absorb it. For this, we would need to repeat facts. That takes us back to the beginning of our book. How do I share information?

> Stories transport implicit, culturally acquired meanings, far beyond the obvious and explicit (Scheier und Held 2006).

Why stories?

- **Stories** help ***to understand and motivate people***.
- **Stories** help ***to learn, remember and share***.
- **Stories** ***motivate, convince, inform and inspire***.
- **Stories** have ***emotional influence***.
- **Stories** substitute for **experiences**.

- **Stories** give **meaning to information.**
- **Stories** provoke no **resistance – advertising does.**
- **Stories are told to be shared!**

Should you still not be convinced that stories are important and the best method to share information or facts, then think of your childhood. How do we teach children not to enter strangers' cars because it might be dangerous?

We read stories to them!

Stories talk to all senses, which lets our memory store them more easily.

A picture paints a thousand words. But a story says more than 1,000 pictures (Simoudis 2004).

Brain researchers talk of "episodic memory" to tell us how important stories are. Our brain has special neuronal networks just for storing and processing stories. All our life events and experiences are stored here, so we can recall them; they severely influence our subconscious behavior (cf. Herbst and Scheier 2004).

Our brain provides a lot of storage space for our own experiences. Our memories are usually accompanied by emotions. We only need to make an experience once to store it permanently (Pöppel 2001).

Take storytelling seriously. Stories are all about the core of a product or service. It only becomes a credible, genuine story if you tell it. So we can say:

► Storytelling is a tool to give life to concepts!

I want to be clear and tell you the relationship between stories and business. What is the goal of a story?

- Share experience (training),
- Share facts (sales),
- Show solutions (everywhere),
- Initiate thoughts (development, etc.),
- Change behaviors (human resources),
- Motivate action (advertising),
- Improve intuition (management),
- Share knowledge (everywhere),
- …

So how do you tell a story? Is there are structure? Stories must of course have a structure to be recognized as stories and stored by our brain. If a part is missing, the story becomes patchy. If we tell too much, it becomes implausible.

The ideal dramaturgy of a story is as follows:

1. One emotional initial situation,
2. A sympathetic main character with influence,
3. Contrast (tensions),

4. Interest through challenges to be overcome,
5. Personal development,
6. Happy ending, comic twist, etc. What do we learn from the story?

The most famous storytellers, apart from our moms and grandmothers, come from Hollywood.

The 22 PIXAR STORY RULES (Price 2011) include one rule about how to concisely tell a story:

#4: Once upon a time there was ___.
- *Every day, ___.*
- *One day ___.*
- *Because of that, ___.*
- *Because of that, ___.*
- *Until finally ___.*

To simplify, we identified the following 10 rules for an ideal storyline.

10 Steps for the Ideal Storyline

1. What is the goal of your story? What do you want to reach?

First we need to ask, for better or worse, what you want to

- Share through your story.
- To what extent?
- What exactly do you want to trigger?

Here, these are three simple questions, but try to define it for yourself or your employees in a few words. Sleep on it for two nights and ask yourself again. Is it still the same goal?

Done? Do you want to share your company's "reason to believe" as a story with your current and future customers? Then let's go to the next question:

2. Which **emotions** do you want to trigger?

Every story has a basic emotion running throughout the storyline.
Another brief summary of the basic emotions:

- Anger,
- Grief,
- Joy,
- Surprise,
- Disgust,
- Fear,
- Love.

This is important so we that do not lose sight of the goal. This shouldn't normally be too difficult, right?

The most exciting task is the third step.

3. Define your protagonists.

Depending on your goal, you will need to use different types of protagonists.

Goal	Protagonist
Trust in leadership	Leader
Activate target group	Target group
Strengthen brand	Product or place
Ask support from target group	Organization

In a novel, you have to define in advance who the protagonist is and what relationships to their environment and enemies should exist. In movies and novels, there are often many actors. All have their own stories, but the storyline revolves around the main protagonist. All other narratives are linked to the main story, but they have to be plausible. For example, movies often insert new stories for individual characters. What is the value proposition?

- You already know the character.
- There are associations we can rely on.

Because there already is a story behind it. Now, what is your story?

4. Find your **story.**

Now, after the protagonist, the emotions and the goal are defined, you can think of a story. For this, you should ask yourself:

- Who am I telling this story to?
- Are there industry-specific topics?
- Are there special places, characters or original stories?

It could make sense to organize small creative sessions and discuss the story or develop the structure for an optimal story, Fig. 3.15.

One possibility is to ask managers and employees to write one page about the company. There are also other options.

1) Try inventing and building a story together. This is the hardest option. The chance of creating an implausible story is high. You should ask professionals to support you.
2) Search and compare all adjectives that you find in various stories. Now you know the basic outline of your story.
3) Take a true story that you found somewhere and develop your story from there. IF you do this, involve the narrator of the original story in your project.

Fig. 3.15 Writing a story

Once you have found your story, let's examine its heart.

5. Describe your **heart!**

A story's heart is not the beginning or the challenges to be overcome. A story's heart is the moment when the protagonist changes their perception and starts on the right path to a happy ending.

The following questions will help you:

- At what moment does everything change?
- What makes the story interesting?
- What were you working towards?
- Which details do you need to tell?

You have to consider whether to deal with *explicit* knowledge (obvious and clear information) or with *implicit* knowledge (information only few individuals can have).

Which information appearing in your story needs explanation? Here, you can often get lost, because readers might not share the author's implicit knowledge.

Try telling your story outside of your team. If the contents work and are understood, you can continue.

If there are questions, you should work more on the story. A story must not leave any open questions. Your readers must be satisfied when they go to sleep.

Therefore: Create a story that leaves recipients WITHOUT ANY QUESTIONS.

It is good to show the heart of a story instead of just talking about it.

SHOW ME YOUR HEART, DO NOT TALK ABOUT IT.

Trust:	For months, your team has been working on an exciting project. But over the last days, your communication has been diminishing. Today at lunch, all your colleagues sat at another table and left you alone. Even your best friend and colleague passed you slowly, looked angrily at you, and went to a different table. What did I do wrong? That's when you know you've done something wrong. Here, I begin to think ... and to understand.
Death:	The ancient telephone in your grandmother's room rings. No one has called her for years. Just then, the grandfather clock begins beating. Its tolling echoes over the telephone. You approach the telephone slowly and pick up the handset. In fearful apprehension, you lift your arm and hold it to your ear. A deep voice tells you: ... An unexpected call (something happened far away)
Lost childhood:	Something in your life is troubling you. You are not satisfied. Your job isn't going too well, your relationship is stalling. Your kids won't listen to you anymore. You feel a broad desire to return to your hometown. As you approach your parents' house, you notice a tree in the right-side mirror. You used to come here as a child. At the house, you park the car and walk across a field, through very high grass, towards the tree, where you played often as a child. The tree seems much taller to you now. It stands on a small hill, with the branches drooping low around the trunk. Then you see something carved into the tree ... Return to a tree (sign of stability)

We've reached the climax. Now comes another, right at the beginning of the story.

6. **Start** with captivating emotions.

The beginning must quickly pull readers or viewers into the story. An emotional start and presentation of the story ensures that they keep reading, start identifying and become interested.

Here's a start you can never go wrong with:

- It started with a journey to ...
- Last week, we got a visit from ...

These sentences usher the beginning of an unusual situation. There is something that attracts us to the protagonist's life.

Always observe the "kitty rule" – Fig. 3.16 – when starting a story. Have you ever played with a kitten? Have you held out a piece of string so that the kitten tried to grab it? The kitty rule says, you should not throw the string too close to the kitten, or it will get bored; but you cannot hold it too far away either, or the kitty will not grasp at it. The goal must be tangible for the kitten.

The same goes for the start of a story. Do not start out too boring, but do not make it surreal either. Find a good balance to keep up the suspense.

Fig. 3.16 Kitty rule

7. What is your happy ending?

A happy ending, a vision, is a reason for most people to continue telling a story.

Tell the story so that it ends well for the protagonist. If you believe you can turn the story around, you should define this in your goal statement. Just make sure that you do not make your listeners and readers unhappy.

Happy ending achieved. Done! Or maybe not. Now comes the main part of the story.

8. Tell the path to realization.

Now it's time to narrate the path from the beginning of the story to its heart. You must build up tension slowly. The protagonist usually has to overcome obstacles, Fig. 3.17. A strong contrast between protagonist and antagonist is very important. Tell about the challenges between the two. The path to realization is the so-called main section, which defines how long the story will go.

Depending on what you want to convey and which group you want to target, your story can last a few seconds or many hours. Will it be a 30-second clip, a novel or just a short story?

Of course you have to be creative! As with the heart of the story, you also have to show the red thread to your audience. In a closed team, you can easily lose your way or develop special knowledge than no one outside your creative circle understands. Therefore:

9. **Test your** stories.

One of the most important elements of storytelling is to test a story. You can use various methods and tools.

- Focus groups,
- Lead user involvement,
- Crowdsourcing,
- Surveys,
- Usability tests,

- Chit-chat.

The simplest, most efficient and fastest method is chit-chat with customers, friends or acquaintances. Tell your story and ask for honest feedback. This lets you quickly develop your storyline, discard or restart it.

Make sure to take your customers' feedback seriously. Do not be stubborn if it is negative. It could increase or destroy your success. Listen to it; and once again:

▶ As long as people ask for clarification, you need to work on your story!
Every question needs an answer.

10. Storyboarding for the **digital world.**

The last step is the storyboard. Draw up the most important situations step by step to prepare them for digital publication. Only then can you decide what tools or media to tell the story with.

The working tool in Fig. 3.18 might help you out.

It asks for the central elements! If you want to tell a story, use the template as a worksheet!

Now, you also know how to emotionalize customers.

Now a summary of the red thread:

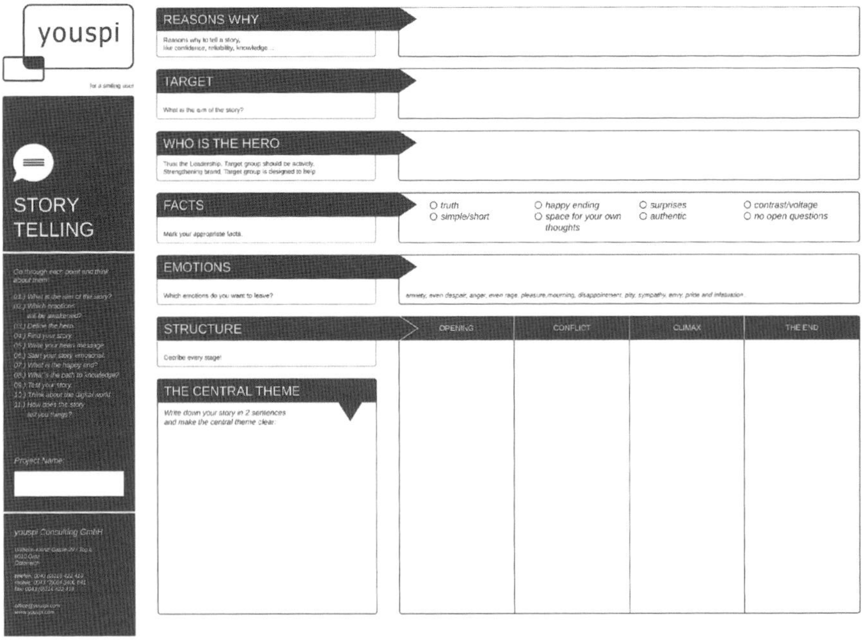
youspi
STORY TELLING
Project Name:
youspi Consulting GmbH
REASONS WHY
Reasons why to tell a story, like confidence, reliability, knowledge ...
TARGET
What is the aim of the story?
WHO IS THE HERO
FACTS
Mark your appropriate facts.
O truth
O simple/short
O happy ending
O space for your own thoughts
O surprises
O authentic
O contrast/voltage
O no open questions
EMOTIONS
Which emotions do you want to leave?
STRUCTURE
Decribe every stage!
OPENING
CONFLICT
CLIMAX
THE END
THE CENTRAL THEME
Write down your story in 2 sentences and make the central theme clear:

Fig. 3.18 Storytelling instructions

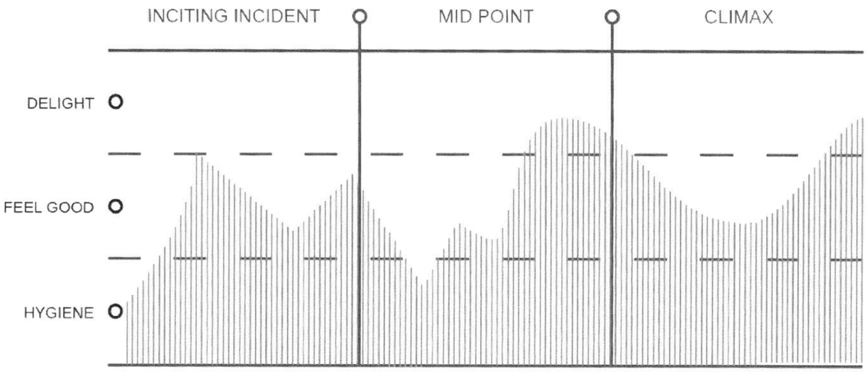
INCITING INCIDENT
MID POINT
CLIMAX
DELIGHT
FEEL GOOD
HYGIENE

Fig. 3.17 Best drama

1. We must **excite** to create **memories**.
2. Memories come from **emotional** experiences.
3. We create them by using **personal** stories.
4. Stories let us create **lasting** memories.
5. Lasting memories create loyalty.

And that's part of ***user experience & customer experience***
In the following chapter, I want to tell you some methods for integrating simplification and emotional appeal into the overall context, into your company or individual projects.

References

Antosik, J. (2011). *Neurolinguistik: Verschiedene Hirnareale für Syntax und Semantik?*. http://uepo.de/2011/10/05/neurolinguistik-verschiedene-hirnareale-fur-syntax-und-semantik/. Accessed 21. April 2015

Friedl (2013). http://tu-dresden.de/die_tu_dresden/fakultaeten/philosophische_fakultaet/ifpw/polsys/lehre/lva/2007/friedel/praesentation1.pdf. Accessed 24.5.2014

Hüther, G. & Nitsch, C. (2004). Kinder gezielt fördern. München: Gräfe und Unzer Verlag.

PepsiCo, Inc., Released: January 2010. http://www.advertolog.com/gatorade/promo/replay-13720655/. Accessed 01.04.2015

Herbst, D., & Scheier, C. (2004). *Corporate Imagery*. Berlin: Cornelsen.

Klein, C. (2009). http://www.sueddeutsche.de/leben/werbung-sex-und-skandal-die-hand-an-der-guertellinie-1.149958-2. Accessed 01.04.2015

http://www.focus.de/digital/internet/das-trifft-ins-schwarze-werbekampagne-nutzt-dressgate-gegen-haeusliche-gewalt_id_4527124.html. Accessed: 01.04.2015

http://marcustroy.com/page/299/?attachment_id=tqxvmirrjbio. Accessed 01.04.2014

http://marketing-gui.de/2010/08/02/hart-harter-hirter-bierwerbung/. Accessed 29 Jan. 2015

Markman, A. (2013). *Ulterior Motives – How goals, both seen and unseen, drive behavior. PsychologyToday*. https://www.psychologytoday.com/blog/ulterior-motives/201005/say-itloud-im-creation-distinctive-memory. Accessed 21. April 2015

Michalko, M. (1994). *Thinkpak*. Berkeley, California: Ten Speed Press.

Pöppel, E.: One-trial-learning. Was ist Wissen? Vortrag anlässlich der festlichen Semestereröffnung an der Universität zu Köln am 19. Oktober 2001

Price, D. A. (2011). *The Pixar Touch*. http://www.pixartouchbook.com/blog/2011/5/15/pixar-storyrules-one-version.html. Accessed 29. Januar 2014

Roth, G. (2001). Neurobiologische Grundlagen des Bewusstseins. In M. Pauen, & G. Roth (Eds.), *Neurowissenschaften und Philosophie* (p. 164). München: Fink.

Scheier, C., & Held, D. (2006). *Wie Werbung wirkt*. Planegg/München: Haufe Verlag.

Simoudis, G. (2004). *Storytising. Geschichten als Instrument erfolgreicher Markenführung*. Sehnert Verlag: Groß-Umstadt.

Zaltman, G. (2003). *How Customers Think: Essential Insights into the Mind of the Market*. Harvard: Harvard Business Review Press.

Methods for Influencing People 4

The simple and emotional buying experience. We have now dealt with the themes of simplicity and emotionality as featured in the title of the book. We have also gotten to the shopping experience in certain themes and areas. But how can we now create these buying experiences across the company in a structured manner? How do I incorporate simplicity and emotionality into the development of my product or service? In this section you will get an insight into methods and overall concepts that you can use for yourself or your company. Bear in mind, however, that process changes or customer-oriented thinking are prerequisites for the utilization of the following methods.

Now I want to tell you how to connect or apply simplification and emotional appeal with methods. We start with the simplification of a process or a service. The methods are called

- Customer journey simplification,
- Customer journey mapping,
- Customer journey innovation,
- Story-centered customer journey.

4.1 Customer Journey Methods

The customer journey is a very simple technique: You put yourself in your customer's shoes and visualize processes or services from their perspective. You cannot adopt your customer's view; it will always be tainted by your own preconditions.

Customers think differently.

Businesses often do not see how complex and unintelligibly some processes and services are structured. Often they do not understand why customers are in a bad mood or why they switch providers. Studies show Figs. 4.1 and 4.2.

See also http://www.allbusiness.com/10-customer-service-mistakes/16569183-11.html, Fig. 4.3.

J. Robier, *UX Redefined*, Management for Professionals, DOI 10.1007/978-3-319-21062-9_4

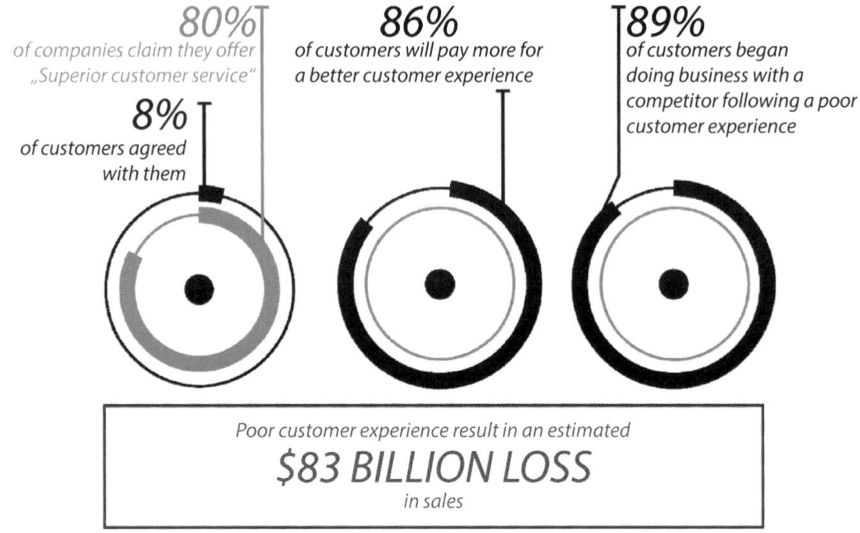
80%
of companies claim they offer
„Superior customer service"
8%
of customers agreed
with them
86%
of customers will pay more for
a better customer experience
89%
of customers began
doing business with a
competitor following a poor
customer experience
Poor customer experience result in an estimated
$83 BILLION LOSS
in sales

Fig. 4.1 AllBusiness Editors (PsychologyToday 2013)

CUSTOMER SERVICE
24% continue to seek out vendors two or more years after a good experience
39% continue to avoid vendors two or more years after a bad experience
62% purchased more
B2B
66% stopped buying
42% purchased more
B2C
62% stopped buying

Fig. 4.2 Study

Fig. 4.3 2D Code to the statistics

See also American Express 2011, Fig. 4.4.

There are processes and services behind every customer service. The customer journey methods were developed to optimize them. They are closely related and intended to be developed in parallel, because they map the same process or service. Before we start, we must define the process itself:

Fig. 4.4 2D Code to the statistics

1. Define the process or service.
2. Define the starting point or the starting points for customers.
3. Define the goal; how will you measure the final success?

How does it look?

4.1.1 Customer Journey Simplification

We start with the quickest, simplest method that can be developed in a workshop.

Of course, each workshop should involve all main process owners. Process owners, service staff and management should get together to achieve a good result.

Interdisciplinarity is a keyword – for innovation!

This will not be possible very often, so I propose working in a small team and then involving the individual key stakeholders.

What does customer journey simplification do?

It visualizes the simplest possible process for the end user, without any of the hurdles that are often necessary out of corporate or legal considerations. And here is how you proceed:

1. Draw the starting point and the goal on a large piece of paper.
2. Now draw the simplest path with all touchpoints, without thinking of external requirements or restrictions.

How does it help us optimize the process?

In the next step, we compare customer journey simplification and real customer journey mapping to simplify the customer journey. Here, you often find simple solutions that are often not considered in regular customer journey mapping. The customer journey map is an important step in customer optimization of processes and services.

Simplification can also mean that you need to integrate an additional interface.

Which number sequence can you grasp more quickly?

1 2 6 9

or

1 2 3 4 5 6 7 8 9

But do not make it a rule to increase functionality at any cost. Because additional information does not always make things easier. Here, MORE numbers are helpful, because our brain has stored the exact sequence from one to nine. But if the sequence went

4 7 1 9 3 5 2 6 8

reducing the numbers would surely make things easier! We cannot predict this sequence, because we have not learned it. You could compare this sequence to complex systems.

An additional interface that needs explanation, even if it explains another, is one interface too much.

It can be so easy and simple; now let's proceed to customer journey mapping.

4.1.2 Customer Journey Mapping

The customer journey map displays the current situation of the process or service. There are clear steps as to how to develop a customer journey map, Fig. 4.5.

1. Define a target group.
   There should be one journey map for each target group.
2. Make observations, record daily diaries and focus groups to understand and recognize your customer's real processes.
3. Define all interfaces/touchpoints.

   There is a special touchpoint analysis shown in Fig. 4.6.

4. Transfer the touchpoints to the customer journey map.
5. Define all actions your customers need to execute.
6. Enter all emotions you identified in the qualitative analysis.
7. Enter all interactions your company needs to perform.
8. Enter all your company's support processes so that the interactions work smoothly. In service design, these mapped out interactions and support processes are also called a "service blueprint". The customer journey and the service blueprint are connected, because it is much more efficient to find a good solution for an overall concept.

Now, you have created a customer journey map. Here, you can compare the customer journey simplification with the current version and you will probably experience a good (or bad) surprise. Now let's look at development and optimization.

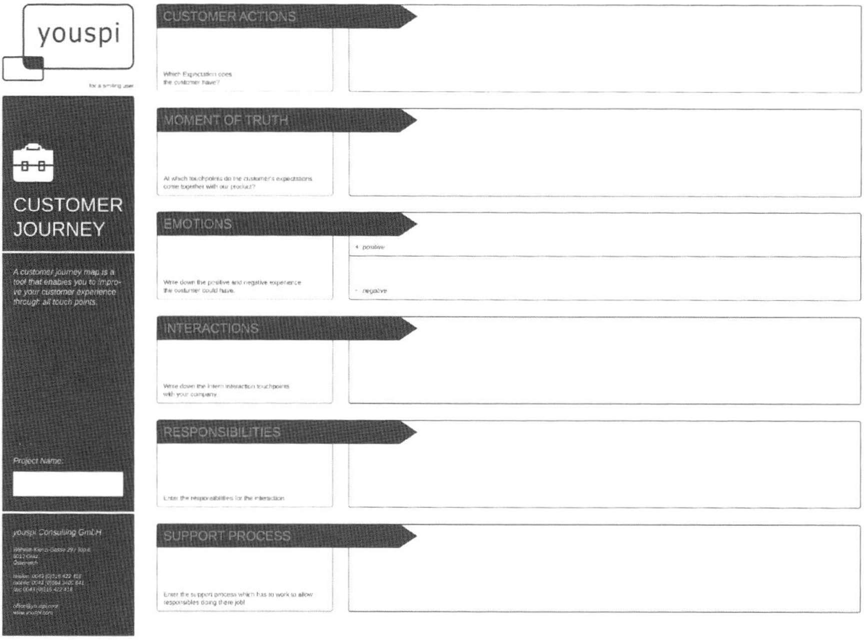
youspi
CUSTOMER JOURNEY
CUSTOMER ACTIONS
MOMENT OF TRUTH
EMOTIONS
+ positive
- negative
INTERACTIONS
RESPONSIBILITIES
SUPPORT PROCESS
Project Name:

Fig. 4.5 Customer Journey Map

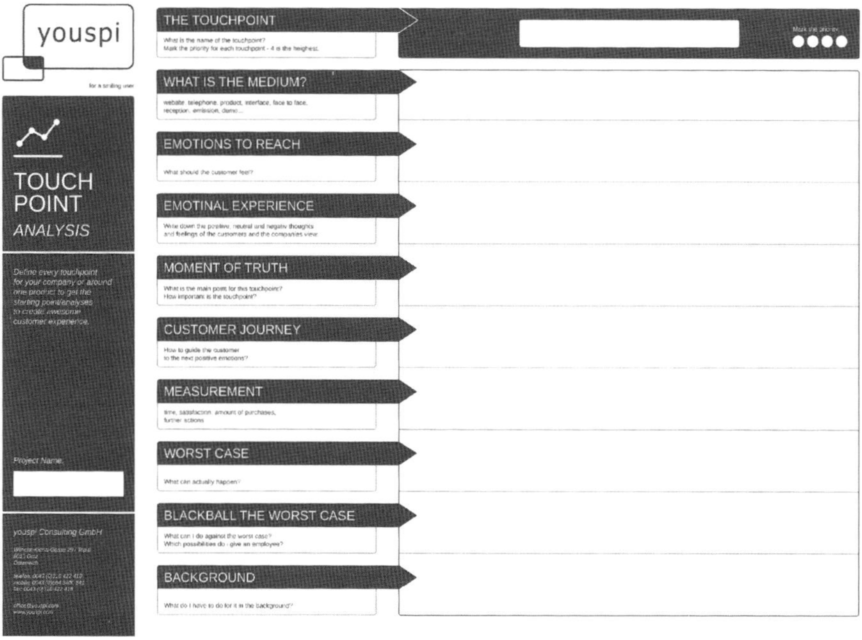
youspi
TOUCH POINT
ANALYSIS
THE TOUCHPOINT
WHAT IS THE MEDIUM?
EMOTIONS TO REACH
EMOTINAL EXPERIENCE
MOMENT OF TRUTH
CUSTOMER JOURNEY
MEASUREMENT
WORST CASE
BLACKBALL THE WORST CASE
BACKGROUND
Project Name:

Fig. 4.6 Touchpoint analyses

4.1.3 Customer Journey Innovation

After analyzing the customer journey map, the status quo, the emotional factors and the customer journey simplification give us hints for customer-oriented optimization. You can only design three types of innovation:

- Process innovation,
- Functional innovation,
- Emotional innovation.

You receive the process innovation by comparing it with the customer journey simplification map. You try to find solutions as to how to adapt the current process of the simplification or how alternative solutions could look.

You can promote targeted emotional innovation if your emotional findings show you a need for optimization.

The functional innovations come from the developments made during emotional and process innovations, Fig. 4.7. Because, as we said earlier, installing new functions that customers do not need makes no sense.

Another option to emotionally capture customers for service processes is the story-centered customer journey.

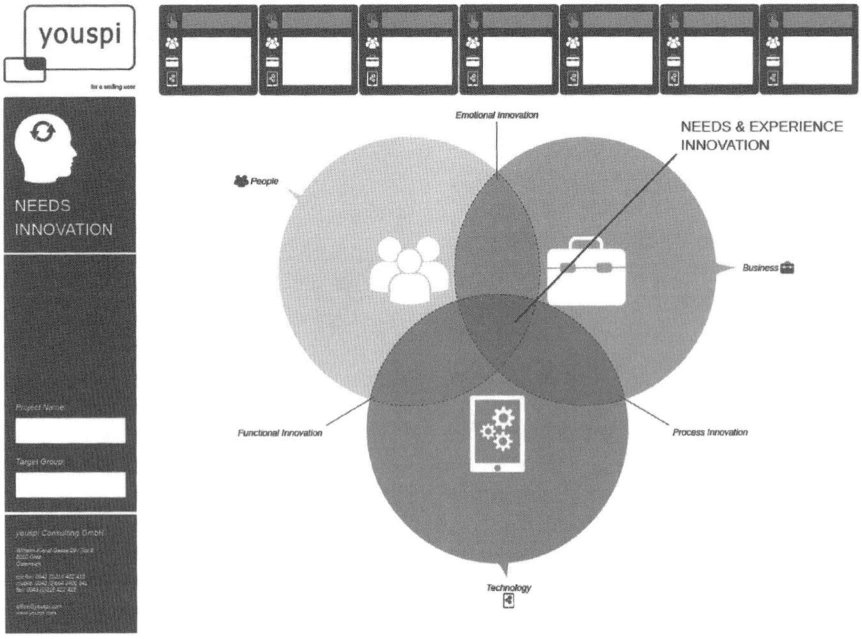
youspi
NEEDS INNOVATION
Emotional Innovation
NEEDS & EXPERIENCE INNOVATION
People
Business
Functional Innovation
Process Innovation
Technology

Fig. 4.7 Needs Innovation

4.1.4 Story-Centered Customer Journey Design

Here, we connect the storytelling technique with a customer journey and lead the customer through the process. An additional dramaturgy, which is integrated into the customer journey, involves them even more in the story. Take your new customer journey map and the storytelling method and try telling a story along your process. Keep adding new information and entertain your customers, so that they want to follow you through to the goal.

1. Create an emotional starting situation.
   Make your customers curious about the story, the product, the process and give them a goal (value proposition).
2. Involve a sympathetic main character and an impact character right from the start. The main character can also be your customer.
3. Establish the contrast. (tensions).
   Depending on how many interfaces your journey includes, you can play around a little.
4. Your journey's challenges arise automatically from the process. Try to make the interfaces more challenging.
5. Develop your customers! (personal development) Tell them their advantages in your story. Teach them your "uniqueness." What is your "reason to believe"?
6. The happy ending, the twist, of course, is the signature, the purchase that signals agreement with your company.
7. In the next step, of course, the product itself needs to work well and be customer-friendly. (Usability/simplicity)
8. Service satisfaction through personal contact.
9. We achieve loyalty and returning customers.

The Needs Innovation Model shows you how to innovatively define steps seven to nine.

4.2 Needs Innovation Model™

Have you ever had the problem to innovate, simplify, and also had to set before your supervisor clear numbers?

The Needs Innovation Model can best be understood as a combination of various established concepts, models and maps, aiming to provide a holistic and reliable way to achieve long-lasting success on the market.

The NI©Model was created to help practitioners gather and assess a comprehensive set of customer needs, thereby determining the critical areas for improvement. In order to identify customer needs and opportunities for value improvement the NI©Model analyses the "Main task & the surrounding journey" that customers are trying to get complete when they use products, services or interact with a company.

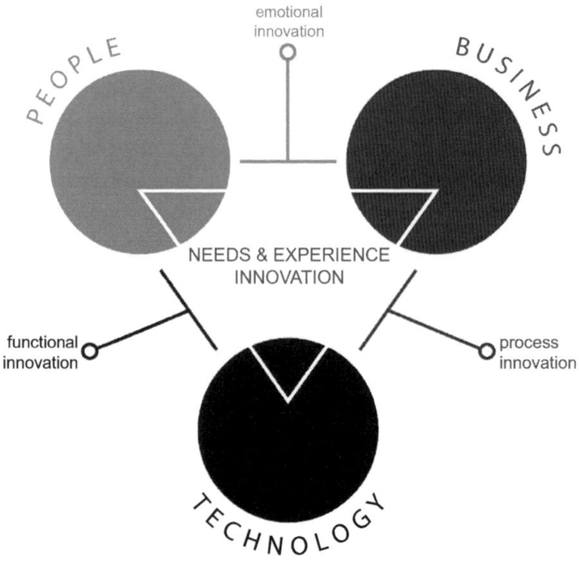
emotional innovation
PEOPLE
BUSINESS
NEEDS & EXPERIENCE INNOVATION
functional innovation
process innovation
TECHNOLOGY

Fig. 4.8 Creating Experience Innovations

The graph shows that you can find "The Needs Innovation or Experience Innovation" in the Center because all methods are combined, Fig. 4.8. This causes that all kinds of innovations are integrated.

A small request on the edge.

BELIEVE in NOTHING

Believe nothing that is "Black on White" as long as you do not try it yourself and have felt for good. Trust your emotions and your logic or your belly.

The Needs innovation model can be used in existing products, as well as new developments. The model is specifically designed for new problems with customer products, processes or services, as it responds to the needs of the end customer.

I want to explain the model through an example. Speech Processing Solution. former Philips Speech commissioned youspi to develop new the Interaction concept of their DPM.

4.2.1 The Model

The seven steps of the Needs Innovation Model are defined as follows:

NI© "NEEDS INNOVATION MODEL", Fig. 4.9

1. Specify the market and the problem.
2. Elicit all needs along the journey in a qualitative research.
3. Quantify needs and ask for satisfaction, importance, KPIs and emotions.

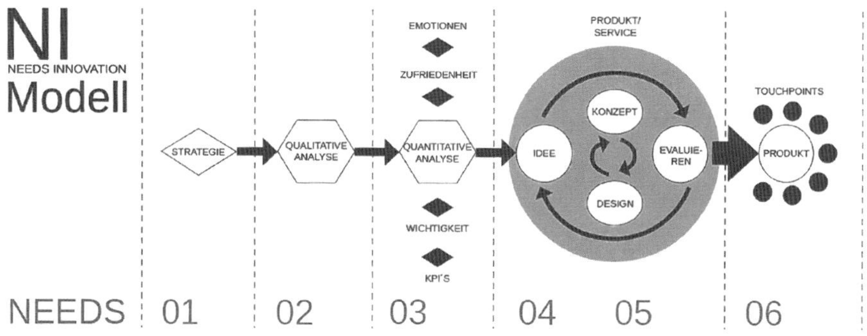
NI
NEEDS INNOVATION
Modell
STRATEGIE
QUALITATIVE ANALYSE
QUANTITATIVE ANALYSE
EMOTIONEN
ZUFRIEDENHEIT
WICHTIGKEIT
KPI'S
PRODUKT/ SERVICE
KONZEPT
IDEE
EVALUIE- REN
DESIGN
TOUCHPOINTS
PRODUKT
NEEDS
01
02
03
04
05
06

Fig. 4.9 Needs Innovation Model by youspi

4. Create the "Needs Prioritization Matrix" and determine the needs with the highest impact and value.
5. Create, iterate, draft and design solutions.
6. Evaluate your new solutions through the previously defined KPIs.
7. Design structured experiences building on the emotions/satisfaction map.

We deployed this model to speech processing systems and redesigned the Philips LFH 9600, Fig. 4.10. It is a high-end device for quality voice recording. Since competitors released new products, Philips had to follow and innovate as well. Through the consequent redesign according to the NI© Needs Innovation Model, Philips achieved an increase of 15 % market share on a global basis with the new Philips DPM 8000.

Furthermore, the model was put into practice to develop, evaluate and optimize a new product for Dewetron, a market leading provider of test and measurement systems showcasing state-of-the-art data acquisition instruments & solutions. Together with Youspi a new multitouch analyzing soft-hardware combination called "Trendcorder" was developed. This product was awarded by NASA as the product of the year 2014 within the industrial sector.

To better illustrate the NI© "NEEDS INNOVATION MODEL", the individual parts of the model are explained below with examples from the Philips DPM 8000 redesign process.

NI© "NEEDS INNOVATION MODEL" used at Philips DPM 8000

Specify the Market and the Problem

At a beginning of every project the first step is an interdisciplinary workshop, where the market and the user group for the envisioned redesigned product are clearly defined. In the case of Philips the following targets were set:

- Optimize the experience for the actual user.
- Enable Philips to enter a new market of analogue voice-recording users.
- Driving market growth within the displacement market.
- Create and integrate 3 core innovations within the redesigned product.

SP
1:23
#3
REC
STOP
PLAY
DPM 9600
KEYWORD
NEW
MENU
VC Voice Command
PHILIPS
DIGITAL POCKET MEMO

Fig. 4.10 Philips LFH 9600 (source: SPS)

It is paramount for the targets to be precisely defined as a first step as this creates the foundation the NI© "NEEDS INNOVATION MODEL" builds up on. With unclear targets, true optimization cannot be achieved, regardless of the effort.

Elicit the Needs Along the Journey

At the beginning the initial user journey for every target group has to be specified in order to define unique user groups for observation and in-depth interviews.

In the case of Philips, Youspi visited lawyers and doctors around Austria and was able to obtain a comprehensive list of various actual needs associated and clustered to the recorder journey. The qualitative study included key stakeholders from 5 hospitals, 5 private doctors, as well as 10 lawyers from different company sizes and their transcriptionists.

All interviews and observations were completed within a 3 week time frame, during which the user input led to valuable insights, in turn enabling Youspi to thoroughly optimize the entire journey.

Recommended methods at this stage comprise in-depth interviews, observations, or daily diary entries. This step is one of the most crucial ones throughout the presented process. Combined with a service blueprint, the needs customer journey map is a tool to evaluate the internal processes.

In the case of Philips, the customer journey was defined through a qualitative user research and completed with internal workshops for the service blueprint. For C-level management qualitative research is often not sufficient, which is why it was decided to quantify the needs of our research studies with 10 times the number of people in our qualitative study.

Some of the identified need are as follows:

Target group	Customer Journey	Need
Analogue user	During recording	data security, no changes
Lawyers	Before buying	High quality product design
Young lawyers	All the time in use	Send dictate to transcriptionist, regardless of the location (Train, home etc. ...)
Lawyers	Tribunal	Long recording time (no possibility to charge)
Hospitals	Before buying	Easy connection to their internal system
Traditional Lawyers	After recording on screen	Fewer, more comprised information
Transcriptionist	Listening to the recorded information	High quality recording
Doctor	Room tour/Visit	Speed

Quantify Needs

As a next step, a large-scale interview phase throughout a time span of three additional weeks was initiated to gather further intelligence for Philips. For the interviews a survey was prepared, which collected

- Satisfaction degree,
- Importance,
- KPIs,
- Emotions

for all clustered needs.

Each interview conducted in this step will last for about two hours and will gather key information on Satisfaction, Importance and Emotions for all needs, which is indispensable to create the Need Prioritization Matrix. The identified Users KPIs are employed to evaluate the optimization of the process at a later stage and are of prime importance for the needs prioritization. This is a great possibility to quantify and prove Usability & User Experience!

Create the Needs Prioritization Matrix

and determine the needs with the highest potential

The "Needs Priorisation Matrix" – Fig. 4.11 – shows all needs with the potential for innovation. Simply put, this means that a high importance and lower satisfaction rate indicate a noteworthy potential. At this stage, a third layer, shown as size and

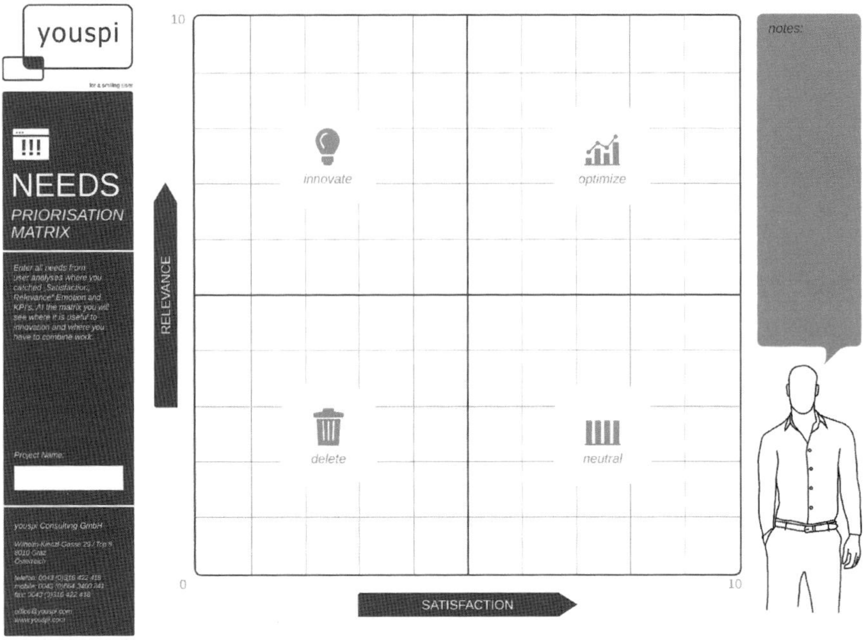
youspi
NEEDS
PRIORISATION MATRIX
Enter all needs from user analyses where you catched „Satisfaction, Relevance" Emotion and KPI's. At the matrix you will see where it is useful to innovation and where you have to combine work.
Project Name:
youspi Consulting GmbH
10
RELEVANCE
innovate
optimize
delete
neutral
0
10
SATISFACTION
notes:

Fig. 4.11 Needs priorization matrix

color of a circle will be introduced, representing emotions, which will ultimately allow you to determine the innovation potential.

It may be possible that some needs have a high satisfaction rate and score low in importance (right graphic area), which enables a possible reduction in functionality or service quality. In fact, reducing unnecessary innovation to create space and simplicity can be a prime way of creating and conveying the added value to the target user, making the product of service itself easier comprehensible, more usable and consequently more attractive for the end-user.

The third dimension "emotion" provides an additional key evaluation possibility on top.

This model thence allows you to concentrate on exactly those needs that exhibit a high acceptance level. In case of the Philips DPM, one prime need for the analogue user was "DATA SECURITY". Users connect a tape with reliability and trust, knowing that their spoken words will be archived and will thence always be available, which is not possible through usage of a digital device. In addition, they know that the recording is happening through looking at the turning tape and thus have a visual input they may be lacking with a digital device.

DIGITAL POCKET MEMO
Index
Menu
Instr
PHILIPS
DIGITAL POCKET MEMO
15/20 DPM 8000.DS2
25:10
01:15:00
Peter Miller
Report
Email
Index
Menu
Instr
PHILIPS

Fig. 4.12 New features, and simulated analogue screen at the DPM 8000 (source: SPS)

Create, Iterate, Draft and Design Solutions for the Needs with the Highest Potential

The next step in the NI© "NEEDS INNOVATION MODEL" is to create, iterate, draft and design solutions based on the previously identified needs with the highest potential.

For Philips, youspi now started its creative processes to define and visualize all defined needs with the attempt to find new technical and User Interface solutions, Fig. 4.12.

Needs	Solution
Analogue user: data security, no changes	Classic mode for clear and simple operation
Fewer, more comprised information	Integrated motion sensor for automatic microphone selection
High quality recording	Integrated motion sensor for automatic microphone selection
Speed	Docking station for quick battery charging and hands-free recording
Speed data security	Integrated barcode scanner for optimization in the documentation

At the iterative development process Mock-UP testing, ergonomic testing and usability optimization testing was included to achieve the best possible solution.

youspi
NEEDS
FEATURE
MATRIX
Fill in the customer´s needs and check how they work with the features.
Projektname:
youspi Consulting GmbH
Wilhelm-Kienzl-Gasse 29 / Top 8
8010 Graz
office@youspi.com
www.youspi.com
USER NEEDS
1.
2.
3.
4.
5.
6.
7.
8.
9.
10.
11.
12.
13.
14.
15.
16.
17.
18.
19.
FEATURES
FEATURES
FEATURES
FEATURES
FEATURES
FEATURES
FEATURES
FEATURES
FEATURES
FEATURES
FEATURES
FEATURES
FEATURES

Fig. 4.13 Needs Feature Matrix

Evaluate Your new Solutions with the Defined User KPIs

As a last step in the usability testing the pre-defined user KPIs were tested and evaluated. The results were outstanding. For the medical use in hospitals the process duration of two days was compressed to a few hours, showcasing a huge innovation in the working process.

During the entire development process all functionalities were checked according to the needs in the previously created needs feature matrix, Fig. 4.13. The needs and functionalities were thence prioritized so the reasoning for the specific design of various processes became clear for all stakeholders. The most important needs had to match the most important features, while being as intuitive as possible.

Design Experiences Building on the Emotions/Satisfaction Map

While the main product, process or service is being redesigned, much more experiences on the base of the "Potential Feeling Map" can be created. Unspoken Needs or less important needs can be complied with fast and easy, while creating additional surprising experiences along the whole customer journey. Such experiences clearly can also be created on the basis of big data. When clustering and combining different target groups, similar needs can be identified, ultimately leading to a tremendous target group.

Experiences may include the following:

- Simple first-use user manual,
- First-use wizard,
- Optimized service delivery.

The NI© NEEDS INNOVATION MODEL provides the tools and a structured process to design, develop and optimize customized products and processes along the entire customer journey.

Given the fact that the NI© NEEDS INNOVATION MODEL relies on both quantitative and qualitative data and is optimizes products, services and processes to suit their exact target audience, end users will showcase very high acceptance rates. At the same time different types of innovations can be achieved based on various identified user needs.

In the case of Philips the following innovations were created:

Emotional Innovations

- Analogue Design,
- First-Use Wizard/Olympus User & Analogue & Non User,
- Product Design.

Functional Innovations

- New scanner tool,
- Improved noise-canceling,
- Automated switching of microphones.

Process Innovations

- Optimized process duration compressed from 1–2 days to a view hours,
- Direct transfer to external transcriptionist.

The procedure and method proved us right where the market was grateful. Within the first six months, Philips achieved a worldwide market share increase of more than ten percent, with further market gains in the subsequent years.

4.2.2 KWB Controller

The controller for KWB biomass heaters is another example of customer-oriented innovation, Fig. 4.14. The redesign started with a dial switch and two pushbuttons for starting and cancelling.

After a stakeholder analysis and the specification of all technical requirements, the company decided to follow the times and add a touchscreen to the new controller. But for efficiency reasons, considering that the target groups were service

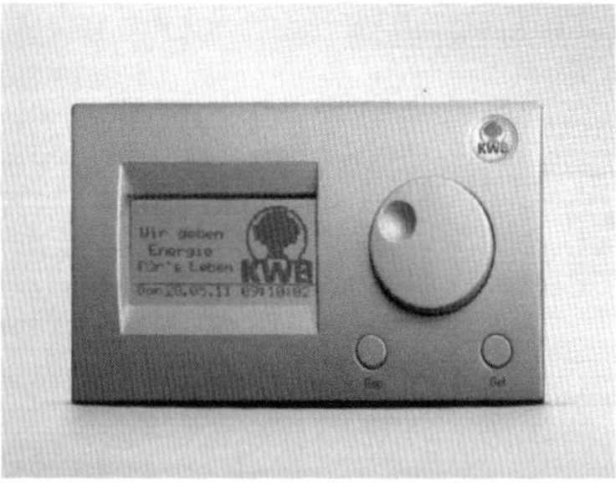
KWB

Fig. 4.14 KWB Comfort3 (source: KWB)

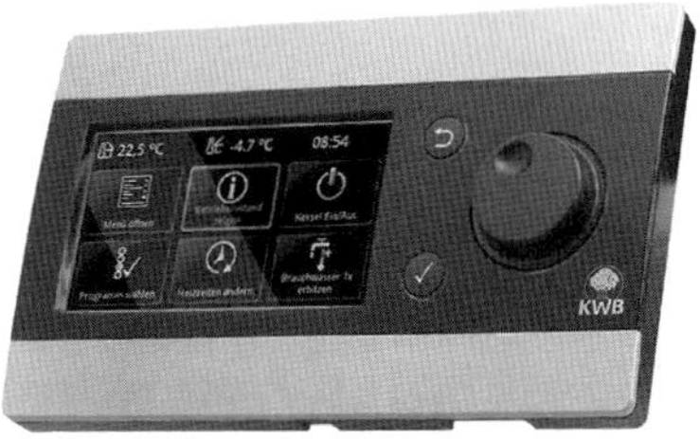
KWB

Fig. 4.15 KWB Comfort4 (source: KWB)

and sales staff, the dial and the two hard buttons were maintained. This hardware concept was also maintained for another reason: Customers find this concept very simple, not just at first sight (see chapter "Simplified human perception"). So the decision was made not to switch to a full touch panel.

The company developed an innovative concept offering three operating modes.

1. Pure touch operation.
2. Pure hardware operation.
3. Combined touch & hardware combination.

Designing the different operating concepts in one panel was a challenge. But this concept was based purely on the needs of different target groups, Fig. 4.15. Customer-oriented innovations have far greater effects than pure technical ones.

All methods and techniques described in this chapter fall into the category of "user experience". I also want to present you the Experience Atlas, as one of several interdisciplinary tools.

4.3 Experience Atlas

This tool visualizes all customer interfaces and their information flows, which are triggered by specific "calls to action". The basic questions are:

- How is information prepared before being sent to customers, how great is their ROI?
- Do your interfaces have a "call to action"?
- Where do they lead?

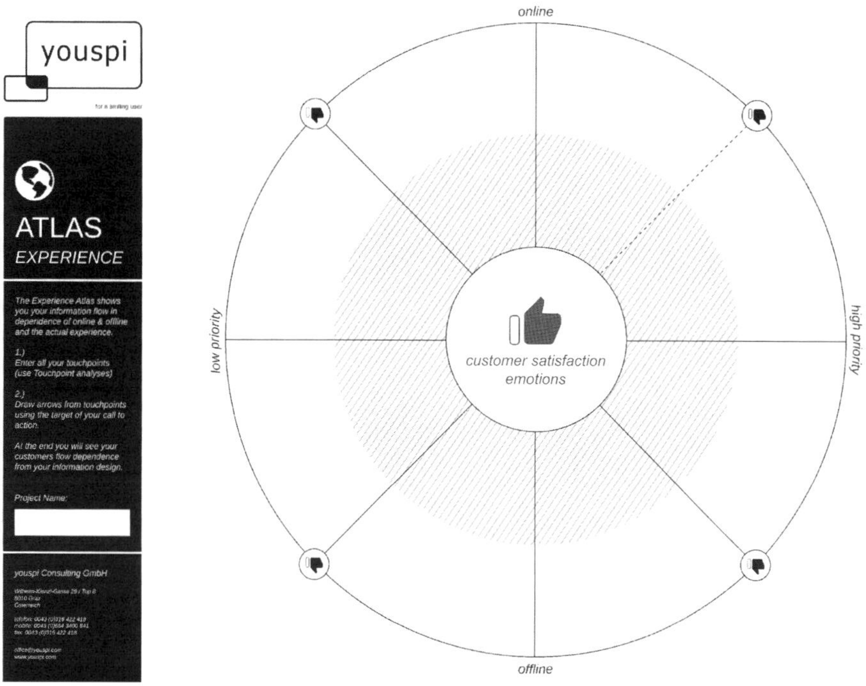
youspi
ATLAS
EXPERIENCE
The Experience Atlas shows you your information flow in dependence of online & offline and the actual experience.
1.)
Enter all your touchpoints (use Touchpoint analyses)
2.)
Draw arrows from touchpoints using the target of your call to action.
At the end you will see your customers flow dependence from your information design.
Project Name:
youspi Consulting GmbH
online
offline
low priority
high priority
customer satisfaction
emotions

Fig. 4.16 Experience Atlas

Have you ever thought about the information flow of your product or service and your advertising material? What do your customer interfaces target, where do they forward customers?

I would use the following slogan to tell efficiency-oriented companies what I mean:

> No information without a **call to action**!

- Whenever a customer interface has no call to action and neglects to show the goal (or points at the wrong one), **your ROI will drop.**
- Whenever this information is not formulated clearly, **your ROI will drop.**
- Whenever these calls to action are hidden, **your ROI will drop.**
- Whenever a customer interface points to several other interfaces, **your ROI will drop.**
- Whenever a customer interface points to nowhere, **there is no ROI at all!**
- Whenever an interface has no call to action, it is useless, and your **ROI also drops to zero**.

The experience atlas shows your customer interfaces and indicates the flow of information. Take your company's touchpoint analysis and draw it into your experience map. The touchpoint analysis questions all the important details that you need to know:

- Online/offline,
- Customer satisfaction with the touchpoint,
- Importance of the touchpoint,
- Forwarded to . . . !

This lets you quickly visualize your information flow and then draw your own conclusions for optimization, Fig. 4.16.

You have now learned many methods for usability, user experience and customer experience. Now, you just need to convince your executives that these are good tools and that they will lead your company to success.

References

AllBusiness (2015) http://www.allbusiness.com/slideshow/top-10-customer-servicemistakes-16569183-1.html, Accessed: 01.04.2015

American Express (2011) Global Customer Service Barometer. http://fonolo.com/blog/2012/03/customer-experience-statistics-2012/, Accessed: 12.04.2015

5 System Customer Persuasion

You have now understood everything and are ready to use the new concepts and methods. But do you now have the problem that you need some like-minded people to work with or still have to convince your superiors? If so, read on and learn the basics of the theory of motivation as a springboard to winning over your target individuals. You will learn how to tackle your comrades-at-arms and get acquainted with some tactics that you can use to convince others of the virtues of usability, user experience and customer experience. To conclude I would like to send you on your way with some studies and statistics that you can include in your presentations.

At first sight, usability, user experience and customer experience are very subjective applications, yet they have great influence on customer satisfaction. These issues are often given an important role, but not an active one. Convincing employees and managers is the first step towards customer-oriented operations. Just getting their agreement is not enough; you have to change corporate structures to efficiently implement customer experience.

To convince customers, let's first see what drives motivation and persuasion, because we need to know how to motivate and persuade others.

This only works if communication is quick, easy and to the customer's satisfaction. Communicate usability – efficiently, effectively and to your customers' satisfaction.

► "Efficient, effective and satisfying usability transfer = user-friendly usability"

5.1 Motivation and Conviction

We usually talk about **extrinsic and intrinsic motivation**, Fig. 5.1.

No matter what job you look at, many people are demotivated and do not feel encouraged by what they do; there is usually one simple explanation:

Managers' motivation techniques just do not work.

Most default motivation tools, like advertising, bonuses, employee of the month awards, interviews or free lunches are just extrinsic motivators. But are they effective?

J. Robier, *UX Redefined*, Management for Professionals, DOI 10.1007/978-3-319-21062-9_5

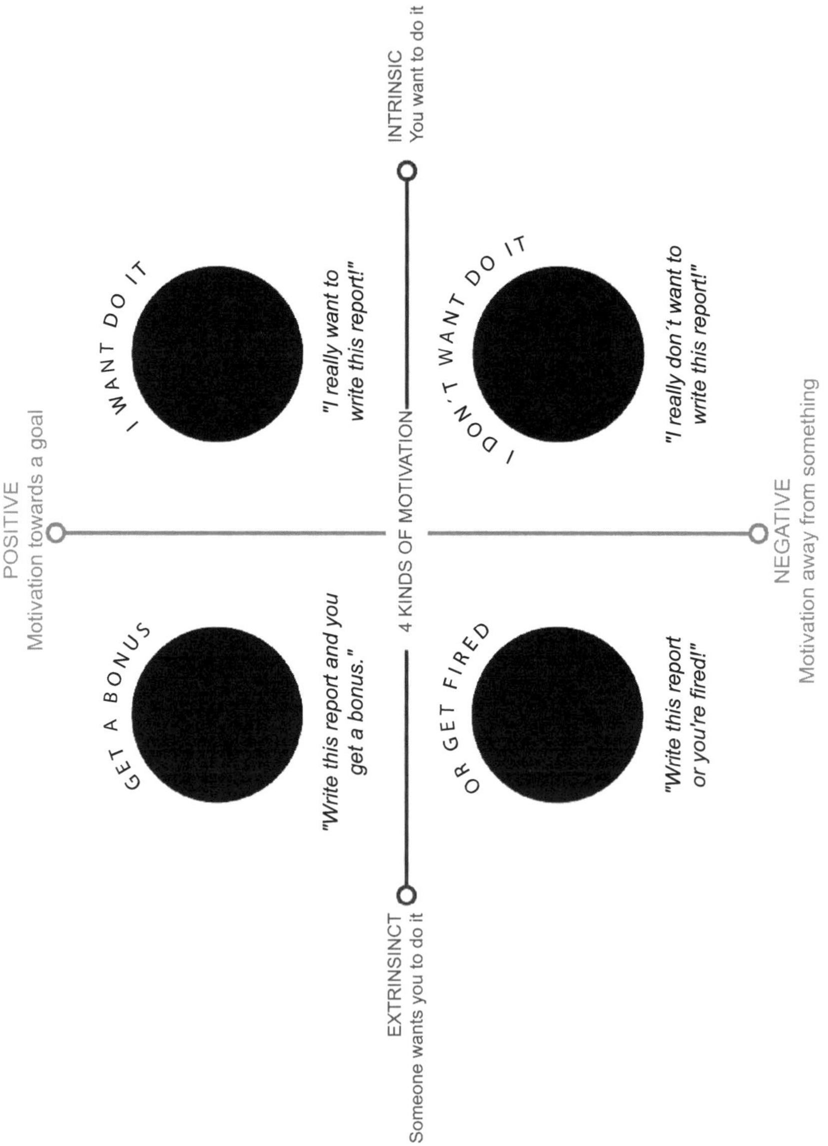
POSITIVE
Motivation towards a goal
NEGATIVE
Motivation away from something
INTRINSIC
You want to do it
EXTRINSINCT
Someone wants you to do it
4 KINDS OF MOTIVATION
I WANT DO IT
"I really want to write this report!"
GET A BONUS
"Write this report and you get a bonus."
I DON'T WANT DO IT
"I really don't want to write this report!"
OR GET FIRED
"Write this report or you're fired!"

Fig. 5.1 Motivation Model

Is it the right tool to motivate people that actually like their job?

Often these wrong incentives cause employees to feel misunderstood. That is plain destructive for their drive, energy and commitment. The following emotions remain (workingamerika 2013):

- I'm being manipulated,
- No appreciation,
- Demotivation.

A Gallup poll shows that 60–80 % of employees are not really occupied at work. Employees feel unappreciated and useless, hence they lack loyalty, passion and motivation. They punch their cards but feel no joy.

There are four types of motivation, but only one quadrant works; unfortunately, managers concentrate mostly on the inefficient ones.

Four types of motivation:

- **Intrinsic motivation** is when you want to do something.
- **Extrinsic motivation** is when someone else tries to make you do something.
- **Positive motivation** is when you want something and have your own goals.
- **Negative motivation** is when you try to avoid something.

Why do extrinsic factors not work? First of all, extrinsic motivation only has short-term effects, if at all. Examples of extrinsic motivation are:

1. Giving sweets to children.
2. Gifts to voters.
3. Pay rises for workers.

A growing number of studies show that these extrinsic motivators are not nearly as good as we thought.

Alfie Kohn has dealt extensively with the topic of motivation and his book, "Punished by Rewards", shows in detail that extrinsic motivation has some serious drawbacks:

1. **They have no lasting effects**: As soon as the punishment or reward ceases, the motivation vanishes.
2. **Their have diminishing effects**: When the reward or punishment stays at the same level, motivation slowly decreases. You will need larger doses of reward or punishment to achieve the same motivation.
3. **It weakens intrinsic motivation**: When the reward or punishment disappears, so does your own initiative to handle tasks.

Kohn uses an example set in a small town, where kids were given points per book that they borrowed from the local library over the summer holidays. They could then swap these points for free pizza. This was an attempt to encourage kids to read.

The children in the program really did read more books than others. But they stopped once the program was over. They now read even less than their peers! Their own desire to read books had been swallowed by the extrinsic reward. No pizza, no motivation to read.

For long-term effects, we can forget about extrinsic motivation.

But negative motivation also has no lasting effect.

Another example by Kohn: Heart patients that had double or quadruple bypass surgeries have a simple choice:

They must stop

- eating unhealthy food,
- smoking,
- laying around,
- drinking alcohol and
- working under stress

or they die.

Paying with your life should be the ultimate negative motivation.

Two years after heart surgery, about ten percent of patients managed to change their lifestyles and lead better lives.

Confronted with the "ultimate negative motivation", nine out of ten people were still not able to make very simple changes in their habits. That is why so many of these heart patients have surgery two or three times. These are strong indicators that negative motivation does not work.

One doctor, Dean Ornish, created a program teaching heart patients to value life and change their habits. They did yoga, meditated, saw anti-stress counselors and nutritionists. The therapy focused on making them enjoy life.

The result: Two years later, 70 % of patients were able to lead healthier lives (Kohn 1987).

If death is no motivation to change your habits, it is clear that motivation based on avoiding things is not as effective as motivation to achieve something. After excluding extrinsic and negative motivation, we only have intrinsic positive motivation to achieve lasting effects (Block and Koestenbaum 2001). This completely changes the role of managers as motivators. Instead of being a source of motivation, the manager must support his employees in finding their inner motivation.

What increases intrinsic motivation?

- **Challenge**: Challenging yourself and completing tasks.
- **Control**: Deciding about what you do.
- **Collaboration**: Achieving something in a team.
- **Recognition**: Positive recognition for your work.
- **Workplace satisfaction**: People that like their jobs are much more likely to develop intrinsic motivation.
- **Respect**: Respecting the work that is done and respecting people. Where there is respect, motivation will rise.

What some managers do not know is that people intuitively want to do good work. Create a positive work environment, and people will naturally develop intrinsic motivation.

Now, we have learned to sell usability and user/customer experience internally and to convince employees or managers to take part.

For managers that are confident, it is easy to enforce top-down decisions. If there is demand and a budget, you can award contracts and hire UX specialists. But what if there is no budget and managers show no great appreciation? You can still drive usability. It always needs people that feel responsible and try to involve others.

Are you such a person?

One person has to deal with usability. Responsibilities must be distributed clearly at the beginning of each project.

The manager must give employees the freedom and time to deal with UX and CX to promote the issue. Now find some opportunities to integrate UX.

5.2 Methods of Persuasion

5.2.1 Quick Stakeholder MAP

At the beginning of each project or before taking a role, fill in a Stakeholder MAP to define what people you will be working with and who you have to involve.

Discuss it with the responsible people.

Your projects will encounter far fewer disagreements, if you clearly define who is responsible for the project and who needs to be involved.

Your first argument could be: "As soon as customers are part of the Stakeholder Map, someone needs to feel responsible and involve them."

This method includes the following intrinsic motivators:

- Control,
- Collaboration,
- Recognition,
- Workplace satisfaction,
- Respect.

Here is how you proceed:

1. Take the Stakeholder Map and enter all people that have contact with the product or system.
2. Discuss with colleagues and key stakeholders.
3. Enter the crucial decision makers, even if they do not work with the system.
4. As soon as you are done, publish the Stakeholder Map or attach it to your door, so everyone can see it.

People that have something to say will make themselves heard. You have set a sign for UX; if it works, you will be able to use tools in the future.

5.2.2 UX Wall

You get a project and know it is not user friendly. To make matters worse, you have no budget to do user research.

Integrate the UX Wall – Fig. 5.2 – into your project. A simple method to remind all project collaborators of UX research and customer integration. This method lets you perform user research throughout the project and find shared solution.

This method includes the following intrinsic motivators:

- Control,
- Collaboration,
- Respect.

Here is how you proceed:

1. Attach the UX Wall where all your colleagues can see it well.
2. Hold an initial workshop, using the Stakeholder Map to define your system's target group and write it into your Wall's first column.
3. Every colleague is asked to attach any UX problems they encounter on the telephone with customers or through the service desk to the Customer Findings columns.

youspi
UX GUERILLA WALL
PERSONAS
CUSTOMER FINDINGS
SOLUTIONS

Fig. 5.2 UX Guerilla Wall

4. Once a week, the findings are structured, organized and, if possible, solved in a designated UX workshop.
5. The solutions should be immediately added to the project requirements.

5.2.3 Fast User Testing

You have already defined the first ideas or concepts. But you do not have the time or money to code it yourself or to order an external usability test? Then just do the test yourself! You only need four to six people to identify most raw usability issues. This will cost you one hour at most.

This method motivates us through

- Challenge,
- Control,
- Recognition.

It is this simple:

1. Draw your concept on a piece of paper.
2. Define two or three of your most pressing questions about the concept.
3. Simply go outside or to your neighbor's office and ask someone for five minutes of their time. If possible, ask people from your target group.
4. Ask your questions.
5. Remember their feedback or write it down.
6. Go back and optimize your concept.
7. Run a second round of tests with all people. For comparison, ask one or two people that are already involved.

But do not ask project participants that are involved in the issue themselves.

5.2.4 UX Brainwashing

As we read about storytelling, the best way to convince someone that usability adds value is to let them experience it. But if you have never cared about usability or your management sees no added value, the next best thing to live experience is a story.

This method could talk to the following intrinsic motivators:

- Challenge,
- Control,
- Recognition,
- Respect.

Here is how you can proceed:

1. Choose one of the following success stories or case studies and …
2. Integrate it into your presentation!
3. Repeat various statements over and over in your company and also give out a call to action, asking your colleagues to try for themselves.
4. Do be aware that you will have to take control.
5. Print out individual stories or studies and attach them in your office or to public notice boards.
6. Post them on your Intranet or use other community tools.

5.2.4.1 User Experience Activities Can Reduce Development Inefficiencies, Fig. 5.3

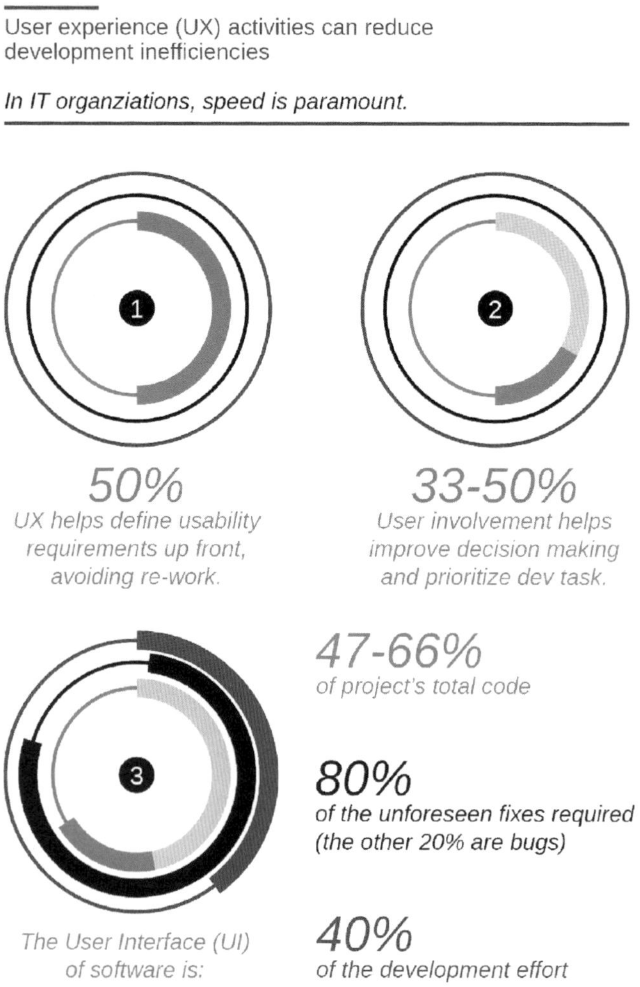
User experience (UX) activities can reduce development inefficiencies
In IT organziations, speed is paramount.
1
2
50%
UX helps define usability requirements up front, avoiding re-work.
33-50%
User involvement helps improve decision making and prioritize dev task.
3
47-66%
of project's total code
80%
of the unforeseen fixes required (the other 20% are bugs)
The User Interface (UI) of software is:
40%
of the development effort

Fig. 5.3 User Experience activities reduce inefficiencies

5.2.4.2 Return on Investments Are Well Documented, Fig. 5.4

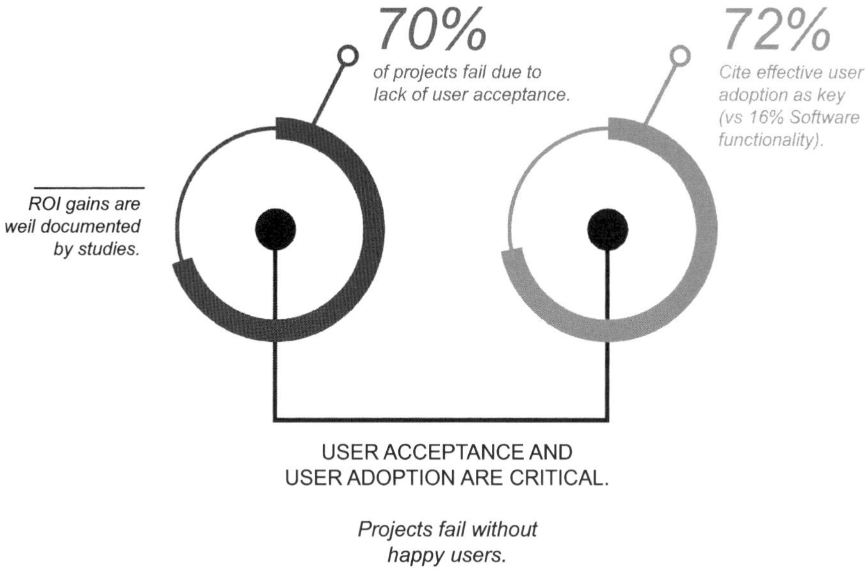
70%
of projects fail due to lack of user acceptance.
72%
Cite effective user adoption as key (vs 16% Software functionality).
ROI gains are weil documented by studies.
USER ACCEPTANCE AND USER ADOPTION ARE CRITICAL.
Projects fail without happy users.

Fig. 5.4 Return on Investment are documented

5.2.4.3 Impact of User Experience, Fig. 5.5

MEASUREMENTS
IMPROVE PERFORMANCE
INCREASE EXPOSURE
GOALS
INCREASE SALES
IMPROVE CREDIBILITY
REDUCE RESOURCE BURDEN

Fig. 5.5 Impact of User Experience

IMPROVE PERFORMANCE

- *Reduce number of user errors*
- *Increase ease of use*
- *Increase ease of learning*
- *Increase traffic/ audience size*
- *Increase number of return visitors when appropriate (retain users)*

IMPROVE CREDIBILITY

- *Increase user satisfaction*
- *Increase trust in the system*
- *Increase number of visits referral*
- *Reduce development costs*
- *Reduce development time*
- *Reduce maintenance costs*

INCREASE EXPOSURE

- *Increase number of new visitors (attract users)*
- *Increase number of visits from search*

REDUCE RESOURCE BURDEN

- *Reduce redesign costs*
- *Decrease support costs*
- *Reduce training needed*
- *Reduce documentation costs*

INCREASE SALES

- *Increase transactions/purchases*
- *Increase product sales*

Fig. 5.5 (Fortsetzung)

5.2.4.4 User Experience Increases KPI, Fig. 5.6

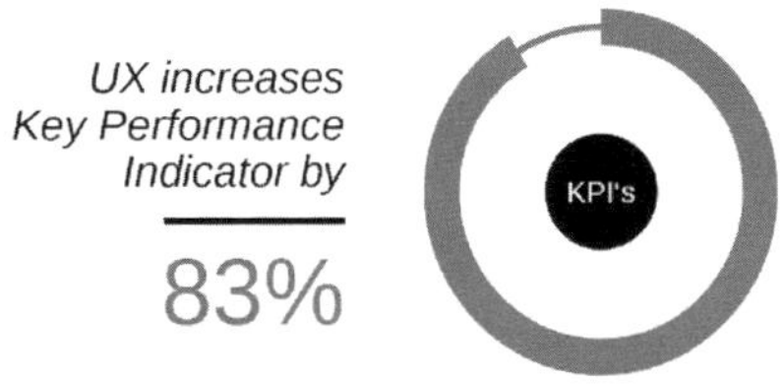
UX increases
Key Performance
Indicator by
83%
KPI's

Fig. 5.6 User Experience increases KPI

5.2.4.5 Proven Investments by User Experience, Fig. 5.7

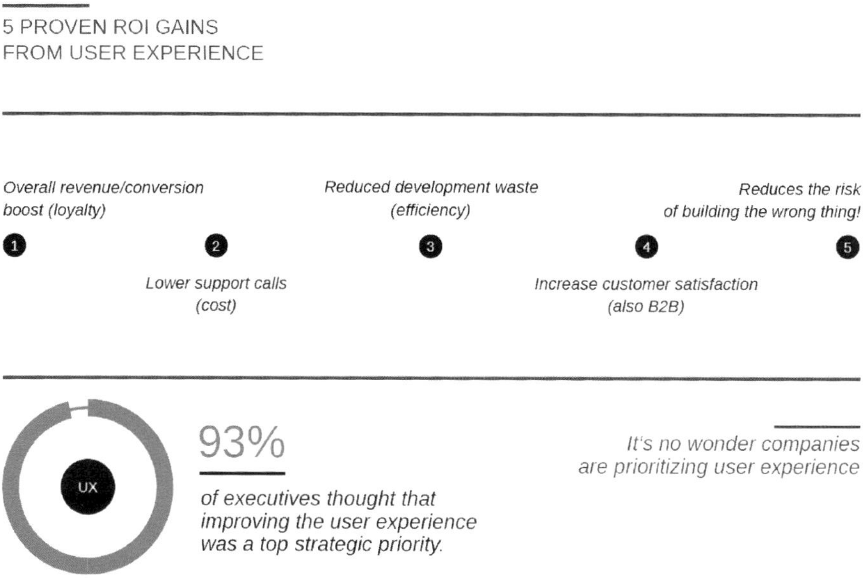
5 PROVEN ROI GAINS
FROM USER EXPERIENCE
Overall revenue/conversion boost (loyalty)
1
Lower support calls (cost)
2
Reduced development waste (efficiency)
3
Increase customer satisfaction (also B2B)
4
Reduces the risk of building the wrong thing!
5
UX
93%
of executives thought that improving the user experience was a top strategic priority.
It's no wonder companies are prioritizing user experience

Fig. 5.7 Proven Investments by UX

5.2.4.6 Invisible ROI by User Experience, Fig. 5.8

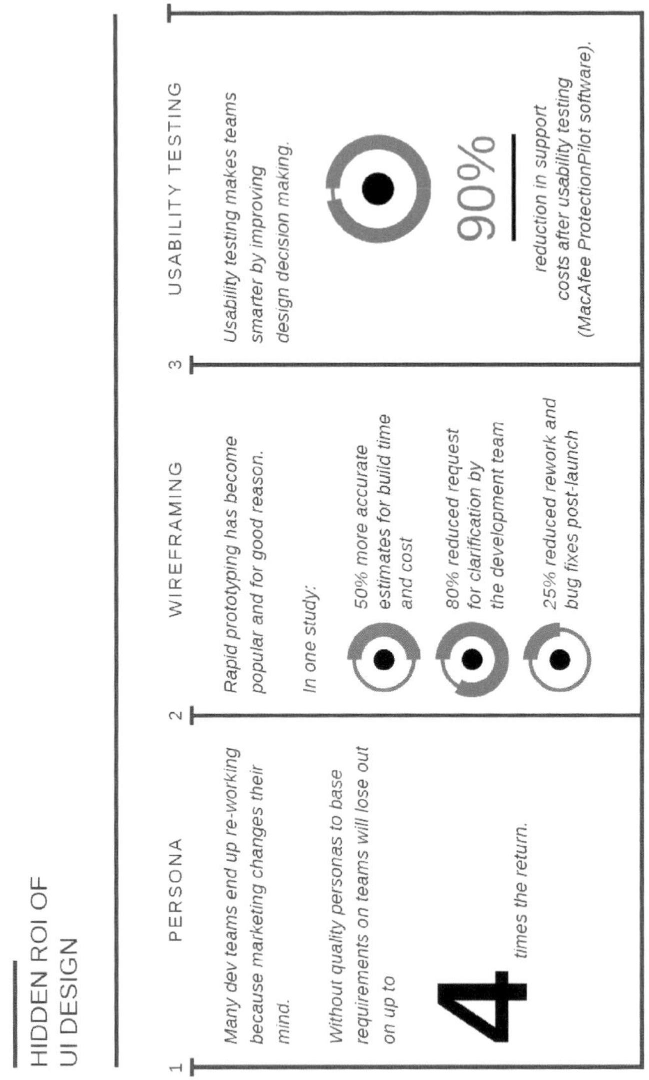
HIDDEN ROI OF UI DESIGN
1 PERSONA
Many dev teams end up re-working because marketing changes their mind.
Without quality personas to base requirements on teams will lose out on up to
4
times the return.
2 WIREFRAMING
Rapid prototyping has become popular and for good reason.
In one study:
50% more accurate estimates for build time and cost
80% reduced request for clarification by the development team
25% reduced rework and bug fixes post-launch
3 USABILITY TESTING
Usability testing makes teams smarter by improving design decision making.
90%
reduction in support costs after usability testing (MacAfee ProtectionPilot software).

Fig. 5.8 Invisible ROI by UX

5.2.4.7 User Experience Leaders Outperform Their Peers, Fig. 5.9

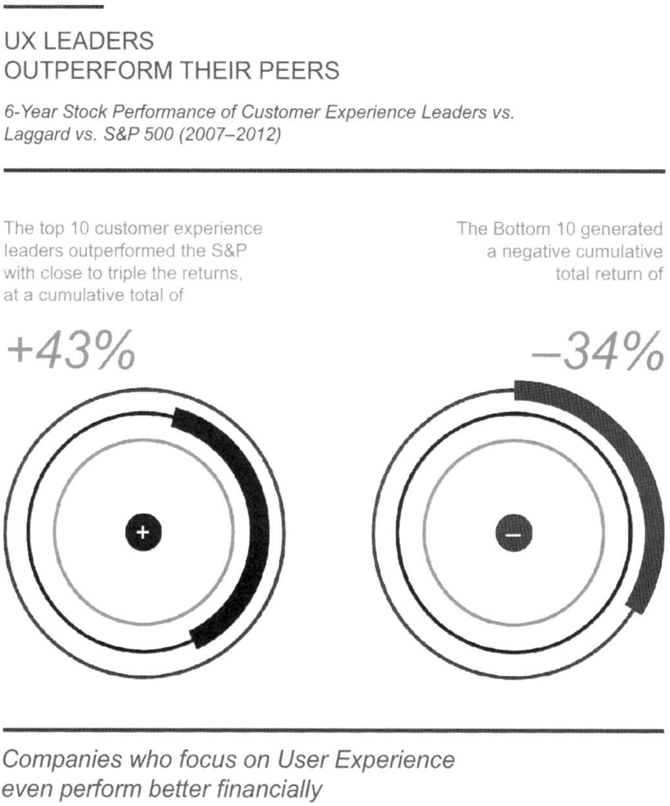
UX LEADERS
OUTPERFORM THEIR PEERS
6-Year Stock Performance of Customer Experience Leaders vs. Laggard vs. S&P 500 (2007–2012)
The top 10 customer experience leaders outperformed the S&P with close to triple the returns, at a cumulative total of
+43%
The Bottom 10 generated a negative cumulative total return of
–34%
+
–
Companies who focus on User Experience even perform better financially

Fig. 5.9 UX Leaders outperform their peers

5.2.5 UX Toolbox

The UX Toolbox – Fig. 5.10 – let you integrate colleagues and managers into the UX process very quickly.

This method could talk to the following intrinsic motivators:

- Control,
- Collaboration,
- Respect.

Here is how you can proceed:

1. Imagine the UX Toolbox in a meeting.
2. Share the methods with your project managers, innovation managers and service owners.
3. Offer to hold an introductory workshop.

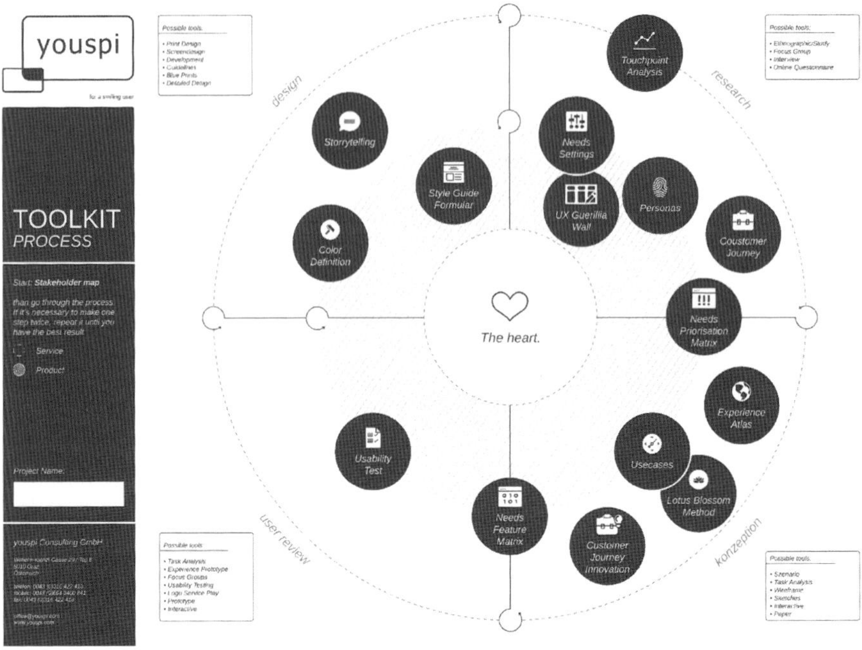
youspi
for a smiling user
TOOLKIT
PROCESS
Start: Stakeholder map
than go through the process. If it's necessary to make one step twice, repeat it until you have the best result
Service
Product
Project Name:
youspi Consulting GmbH
Possible tools:
• Print Design
• Development
• Blue Prints
• Detailed Design
Possible tools:
• Task Analysis
• Experience Prototype
• Focus Groups
• Usability Testing
• Logo Service Play
• Prototype
• Interactive
Possible tools:
• Focus Group
• Interview
• Online Questionnaire
Possible tools:
• Szenario
• Task Analysis
• Wireframe
• Sketches
• Interactive
• Paper
design
research
user review
konzeption
Touchpoint Analysis
Storrytelling
Needs Settings
Style Guide Formular
UX Guerillia Wall
Personas
Coustomer Journey
Color Definition
The heart.
Needs Priorisation Matrix
Experience Atlas
Usability Test
Usecases
Lotus Blossom Method
Needs Feature Matrix
Customer Journey Innovation

Fig. 5.10 UX Toolbox

Fig. 5.11 Download Data

This lets you bring usability to your company. The first techniques will be used in your company soon.

Download all statistics and a part of the toolbox under the following link: www.youspi.com/uxredefined/UXToolbox_youspi.zip, Fig. 5.11.

References

Alfie Kohn: http://naggum.no/motivation.html, Alfie Kohn, a Cambridge, MA writer, is the author of "No Contest: The Case Against Competition", recently published by Houghton Mifflin Co., Boston, MA. ISBN 0-395-39387-6 accessed: 03.12.2014

Block, & Koestenbaum (2001). *Freedom and accountability at work, by Peter Block and Peter Koestenbaum.* San Francisco: Pfeiffer.

Gallup (2014). *Gallup.* http://www.gallup.com/de-de/181871/engagement-index-deutschland.aspx. Accessed 01.02.2015

workingamerika MyBadBoss contest, http://www.workingamerica.org/badboss/index.cfm?appState=winners. Accessed 12.05.2013

6 The Simple and Emotional Selling Proposition

The Reason to Believe exposes the most important reason to buy and the underlying sales argument. The Reason to Believe wants to provide actual or subjective facts to affirm customers' purchasedecision http://de.wikipedia.org/wiki/Kaufentscheidung and make them feel well about the product beyond the purchase process.

The Reason to Believe is not equal to a product's unique selling proposition, but it can also be the same.

Usually, it is not the additional functions that tell our brain whether a product is worth buying. It is the emotional links, as well as simplicity and efficiency. Your company will always have an overall image that influences your Reason to Believe.

- Think holistically.
- Think emotionally.
- Think simply.
- And communicate it!

J. Robier, *UX Redefined*, Management for Professionals, DOI 10.1007/978-3-319-21062-9_6